ABOUT THE BOOK

As founder and CEO, you're used to making all the decisions, but the business you have isn't yet the one you envision. You need a COO—someone who can help build the company you don't know how to build on your own.

The Second in Command is your go-to guidebook when you're ready to scale up. Cameron Herold details every aspect of the process, from knowing when you need to hire a COO, through identifying and hiring the right candidate, to successfully onboarding and working with them.

The Second in Command reveals the benefits COOs bring to companies and explores the many ways a COO mastermind or COO forum can help grow your COO's skills. You'll meet the different types of COOs and understand the role each type plays. Discover how to bring a COO into your company with the least disruption and avoid common problems before they arise. There is no need to go it alone.

ADVANCE PRAISE

"Reading this book twelve years ago would have saved us both from hiring the wrong COO at least five times. We didn't know there were so many different types of COOs and so many roles they could play, which led to unclear expectations and imminent disaster. If you need a second command and want to avoid the mistakes most founders make when hiring one, then reading The Second in Command is simply essential."

—HOLLIS CARTER, CO-FOUNDER, THE
BABY BATHWATER INSTITUTE

"Cameron is not only an inspiration, but the best example of what a COO represents. The Second in Command is a critical read for any organization looking to scale to a substantial exit value. Cameron's understanding of the COO role is wisdom every CEO will want to have if you're looking to sell your company. This is a book I will refer our clients to time and time again."

—ROB FOLLOWS, CEO, STS CAPITAL PARTNERS

"If ever there was a patron saint of Chief Operating Officers, it would be Cameron Herold. He has a unique understanding of the role and its relationship to the CEO, imparting practical techniques to make sure that these two can work in concert to turn ideas into reality effectively. To any CEO and COO looking to create an organization and culture built through intention and design as opposed to by accident: do yourself a favor and connect with Cameron's work."

—DARREN VIRASSAMMY, COO, CFO AND
CO-FOUNDER OF 34 STRONG, INC.

"Cameron's approach makes business simple in a complex marketplace. He has saved us time, money, and headaches numerous times. Most importantly, he helped position our team for growth so that we can drive toward the vision of our brand at lightning speed. You won't regret a minute of time you invest in learning from him, and I am certain your team will feel the same. Mine sure does!"

—ANDREW FRASER, CEO AND FOUNDER OF DOGIZONE

"I have been incredibly fortunate to have met and worked with Cameron Herold on several levels—professionally and personally, in person and virtually. His deep understanding of the CEO and COO relationship is simply astounding. He understands the proverbial yin and yang relationship necessary, while also understanding the unique intricacies that make every organization and every dynamic duo different. This book is an intense coaching session—in the palm of your hand—that will transform your business if you put the work in to execute on Cameron's principles."

—LINDSAY SMITH, CSO OF TITLE ALLIANCE, LTD.

"Here Cameron goes again, with another timely and insightful book focused on a critical area of business that is too often overlooked. Cameron brings all of his practice, personality, and prowess to bear in this excellent book. I continue to learn from him, and this is no exception. A must-read!"

—GRAHAM BRODOCK, PRESIDENT OF KRISTECH WIRE

"Cameron Herold completely understands the value the COO role brings to an organization. His compass is spot-on for what type of COO a chief executive needs, why they need it, and when. This book is required reading for CEOs who are serious about building out their leadership teams."

—SCOTT SHRUM, PRESIDENT AND COO
OF HENNESSEY DIGITAL

"Pragmatic and with a wealth of experience, Cameron Herold brings actionable and effective wisdom you'd be foolish to ignore. Conversational style—easy to read."

—JEN LEECH, CO-FOUNDER, PRESIDENT
AND COO OF TRUSSWORKS, INC.

"Cameron's mastery in the COO landscape is second to none. For every CEO questioning whether they need a COO or if their COO is the right person, this book has your answer."

—KELLY CLEMENTS, COACH, SPEAKER AND AUTHOR

"Finally, a book comes along that accurately depicts the unique dynamic between CEO and COO—a marriage between executives. And, more importantly, it provides clear insight into the full scope of the COO role and the diversity that exists within it. The value of a COO can't be overstated... This book explains why COOs are the linchpins of an organization."

—BRAD KOSSOWAN, COO OF AVEIRO SLEEP LP

"Another absolute mic drop from Cameron Herold!

"Cameron's hands-on expertise allows him to share real-life knowledge and practices with the reader like very few in the world can do. This is not your ordinary business book; this book is your guide to breaking out your COO like you've never imagined."

—LUKE MILLIGAN, GENERAL MANAGER
OF ZEN WINDOWS COLORADO

"This book is a breath of fresh air that sheds light on the second-in-command; also known as the COO. Oftentimes, the COO gets forgotten, but Cameron and his principles in this book will change how COOs operate and are viewed in the future. If you are a leader of an organization, this is a must-read from one of the top business mentors of our time."

—CLINTON SENKOW, MANAGING DIRECTOR
OF SENKOW VENTURES

"'Leaders are Readers,' and once again Cameron Herold helps teach what others won't or can't. This newest installment provides us with thoughts that can easily become our words; and then those words can become our habits, and finally, those habits can enable any and all COOs to speak with integrity and be impeccable with their words—regardless of the company, role, or scope of responsibilities they have."

—GEORGE J. HORVAT, COO OF AGERO, INC.

"I cannot imagine leading JAM without my right-hand, my integrator, my COO. He is the brake to my gas pedal, the thunder to my lightning... He keeps our business focused on what matters most! And I cannot imagine turning to anyone but Cameron to learn more about how best for a COO and CEO to work together. Cameron has experience as a COO and has had years of coaching some of the best CEOs and COOs in the world."

—KRISTI HEROLD, FOUNDER AND CEO
OF JAM SPORTS & EVENTS

"The day I brought on my new COO, I told him two things: 'welcome to the team,' and 'go learn from Cameron.' Cameron has the unique ability to not only execute at the highest level of business, but also to communicate exactly how he does it. That's why I was so excited for this book—and why I'm recommending it to all my CEO friends. Cameron's books have made such a profound impact on my life and business, and this book might just be his best yet."

—BRANDON TURNER, FOUNDER AND
CEO OF OPEN DOOR CAPITAL

"Cameron has so much knowledge and experience, and so many connections in the business world, and he's really utilizing all of that to help both the CEOs and COOs of the world turn their vision into a reality. This book is not only great for CEOs, but also for current and aspiring COOs who want to understand how to maximize their impact."

—CLEMENS KIM, COO OF CLORE BEAUTY SUPPLY

"It's rare that someone knows how to speak to both CEOs and COOs. Cameron has done it with this book. It truly spoke to me. Having my COOs in COO Alliance has me realizing the best CEO/COO combinations are made (and practiced) more than they are found. Cameron's book is a must-read for both CEOs and COOs who want their relationship to be great."

—DAVID BERG, CEO OF REDIRECT HEALTH

"If you want your company to run with greater productivity and efficiency and less stress—you need to read Cameron Herold's The Second in Command: How to Unleash the Power of Your COO. Being a visionary myself, the operations side of the business is not my strongest skill, so I follow Cameron's advice. I've seen the impact he's created in the companies he's worked for and with, including many brands you would recognize and numerous successful entrepreneurs I know personally. Because of that, I've implemented many of his strategies and tactics in my own business and have seen tremendous improvements as a result. His advice is priceless."

—JEREMY KNAUFF, FOUNDER OF SPARTAN MEDIA

"Cameron's lived, coached, and mentored experience around CEOs and their 2IC makes him the perfect author to write a book on this critical part of every business's success. It always takes two, and finding your second-in-command is key to scaling any business."

—MITCH DODD, COO OF KINTEC

"*Cameron does it again! The Second in Command beautifully unlocks the mysteries of the COO role. Not only does it help you, as CEO, identify who's best suited to be your Number Two, but it also gives practical insights on how to further empower them to lead your company to new heights. It's a jam-packed, to-the-point must-read for any CEO with a vision.*"

—PARCHELLE TASHI, FOUNDER OF THE AUTHOR'S LEVERAGE

"*When I first came into my family's business four years ago, my role was to fill the gaps. I had very limited experience with many of the challenges I would face. Beginning with reading Double Double, and then bingeing on Second in Command Podcast episodes, and finally joining the COO Alliance, I have been able to find many of the key resources I need. This book is another tool in the toolbox that can build a framework around the thinking of operating an organization.*"

—TIM DUFFANY, OPERATIONS, DUFFANY BUILDERS

"*Cameron Herold makes a strong statement on the Why for a second-in-command, and on the importance of the COO role in the growth of an organization. I have much respect for the COO position—which I have treated as a CEO role split in two, with the CEO driving the strategy and the COO the overall operations...vital to any organization. However, Cameron explains the COO styles and rules of engagement for a strong governance.*"

—FRANÇOIS PLOURDE, CEO OF CIMA+

THE SECOND IN COMMAND

CAMERON HEROLD

THE
SECOND IN
COMMAND

Unleash the Power
of Your COO

LIONCREST
PUBLISHING

THE SECOND IN COMMAND
Unleash the Power of Your COO

FIRST EDITION

ISBN   978-1-5445-3762-7   *Hardcover*
       978-1-5445-3760-3   *Paperback*
       978-1-5445-3761-0   *Ebook*
       978-1-5445-3763-4   *Audiobook*

To my wonderful two boys, Aidan and Connor: I love you more than you know. I think of you and cheer for you every day. I hope that when people ask, "What does your dad do?" you tell them about what I do for fun, and where I travel to. I don't want to be known just for what I do or did for work.

To my wife, Ashley: you wow me, you inspire me, and you really do make me a better person every day. You're one of the very smartest, most driven, and most wonderful people I know. Thank you for all the gifts your love has given me. And thank you for being my partner in, and documenting, our bucket-list life.

CONTENTS

FOREWORD 19

INTRODUCTION 23

PART 1: COOS: A USER'S GUIDE

1. WHAT IS A COO? 33
2. WHAT'S THE POINT OF A COO? 51
3. WHY HIRE A COO? 75
4. DO I NEED A COO? 89

PART 2: HIRING A COO

5. STARTING THE PROCESS 99
6. HOW TO HIRE 111

PART 3: WORKING WITH A COO

7. ONBOARDING 143
8. WORKING TOGETHER 171
9. WHAT DO I DO NOW? 189
10. THE PARTY'S OVER 203

PART 4: APPENDIX

SECOND IN COMMAND PODCAST: THE TOP TWENTY-ISH .. 211

COO ALLIANCE 213

SAMPLE COO SCORECARD 217

A COO MANUAL 221

FURTHER INFORMATION 227

ADVICE FOR COOS FROM COOS 229

ACKNOWLEDGEMENTS 235

ABOUT THE AUTHOR 237

FOREWORD

I remember I was stuck.

My business was not growing beyond $1 million. I was the vision guy, but I needed an executor. Someone who could turn my vision into an orchestrated reality. I remember attending an Entrepreneurs' Organization event in San Diego where the keynote speaker spoke about a model called "two in the box." The idea was simply that two heads are better than one. You often have an entrepreneur who is really great at seeing big ideas and imagining the magic, but—because they are easily distracted by the next shiny object—they have a harder time making the magic happen. That's when they need a second head.

I had met Cameron Herold through my Entrepreneurs' Organization forum group. He was between jobs, and I used to talk to him over beers about the challenges I was having "un-sticking" myself from myself. I was getting in my own way. Cameron loved reverse- engineering the future and figured he could help.

Cameron and I were both fire-ready-aim types. I could see big things and get excited about them, but I needed Cameron to organize my ideas and fire quickly. To take action.

We were a new brand in a very fragmented category, and we needed to move fast to establish 1-800-GOT-JUNK? as the market leader. Cameron could rally the team and get them excited about our ideas, and he had the leadership and management tools that would help him scale the team into action quickly.

Cameron was amazing! He helped take the company from $2 million to over $106 million in just seven years. There is no way I could have built half the company I built without him. Not only did we have fun together, but we were each other's yin and yang. We were the right team to get us to $100 million... but not beyond it.

As the company grew past that magical milestone, we needed a new level of rigor and discipline. It was time to recruit a new second-in-command. This time, I over-hired, and the biggest mistake I made was abdicating my responsibility as opposed to delegating a clear vision to this new leader. Just fourteen quick months later, the relationship ended. I had failed.

Unclear on my next steps, I reached out to a longtime friend and mentor, Greg Brophy, the founder of the multi-billion-dollar brand Shred-It. He said, "Listen Brian, it's like Goldilocks and the Three Bears. The first time you hire someone close to you—a friend like Cameron—and it works like magic. The second time, you over-hire and you bring someone onboard based on pedigree versus cultural fit. The third time, you need to get it right. You need to find someone who has the rigor and discipline but also believes in and wants to work with an entrepreneur."

I couldn't afford to fail again. I put the word out to my network. I created a painted picture—what Cameron calls a Vivid Vision—of exactly the person I was looking for. I was so detailed that three unrelated people around the world came back to me and said, "There's only one person who fits what you describe. And that's Erik Church."

This time, I took my time...We courted each other for ages to ensure the fit would be right. I saw that Erik had always worked with an entrepreneur. He understood the challenges and possibilities of that relationship.

It has been absolute magic! Erik has taken us from $100 million to well over $600 million...and soon to be $1 billion.

While I'll always love and appreciate Cameron, he would be the first to tell you he wasn't the guy to take it to the next level. And that's what you need in a COO: the right person, at the right time, working with the right vision.

—BRIAN SCUDAMORE
FOUNDER AND CEO OF 1-800-GOT-JUNK? AND O2E BRANDS

INTRODUCTION

Every CEO has a vision of growing their company or running it better. But for most, the vision is as far as it gets. As the company starts to grow, so do the CEO's problems. They can't seem to hire the right people or grow their team. They don't have time to execute on their growing list of urgent, high-impact projects. They can't even think of positioning the company to sell.

Many CEOs get stuck in the day-to-day instead of building the overall business. They have no time for strategic thinking. They spend too much energy working on too many areas where they kind of suck, which leaves them feeling drained. And that just makes the problems worse. Other CEOs may be great at the details but would rather have someone else actually dealing with the details on their behalf, so they can focus on more strategic areas, or on areas that energize them.

Most CEOs I've met know exactly what I'm talking about.

It's enough to make even the most visionary CEO feel over-whelmed. The good news is that, though you might feel like you have to do everything yourself, you don't. You just need to hire the right second-in-command. That's often a COO, although (as we'll see) there are a number of titles that all describe a similar role, any of which can achieve the same results. Mostly, though, I'll use the term COO as a shorthand.

If you can find a COO who complements your skillset, the partnership will set your business on fire. You won't be by yourself anymore. That alone is a huge change that will give you space to be strategic again. In many ways, you will be one of two in the box on the org chart. And the power of two doesn't just double your effectiveness. It multiplies it exponentially—and it brings the Vivid Vision that inspires you within reach.

The bad news is that hiring the right COO isn't easy. And hiring the wrong COO is worse than useless. It can kill your momentum...or your company.

This book will help you avoid mistakes. It will show you how to find the right COO for you and for your business, whatever stage you're in. It will help you figure out the kind of COO you need, and tell you where to look for them, how to hire them—and how to work with them to bring your vision to life.

I've stepped in to help three CEOs realize their visions by growing their companies to over $100 million. The highest-profile occasion was when my best friend Brian hired me to help him grow his small junk-removal company, 1-800-GOT-JUNK?. He believed it could scale rapidly, but he couldn't do it on his own. With him as CEO and me as COO, we grew the company from $2 million to $106 million in six and a half years.

Brian couldn't have fulfilled his long-term vision without me—and I couldn't ever have been an effective COO without him. Brian was the visionary, and I was in the trenches. It was hard as hell, but I was in heaven. We were yin and yang. And, in many ways, we were even stronger than the EOS Visionary and Integrator that so many talk about. We had a bit of an unfair advantage, as he'd been best man at my wedding three months before I joined him as COO. We also did a lot right, which I'll uncover throughout this book so you have the same upside.

In 2008, I spoke at a conference run by the founder of the Entrepreneurs Organization, Verne Harnish. As I left the stage, one of Verne's coaches, Kevin Lawrence, walked up to me and said, *"Wow!* I thought you were a saying, but you're a real person!"* For two days he'd heard entrepreneurs at the Gazelles (now Scaling Up) conference saying, "I need a Cameron." He figured it was a business term, like "I need a Flywheel" or "I need a BHAG."

My name had become shorthand for someone who can execute a vision and help a CEO grow their company. What the entrepreneurs were really saying was that their business was missing a piece; they needed a COO. And many of them likely did—but they didn't need a Cameron. For at least 90 percent of the CEOs at the conference, I would have been a terrible COO. I wouldn't have matched them or their needs. It would have been a disaster. In fact, when I think about all the members of the COO Alliance, an organization I set up and still run to support elite COOs from around world, I likely couldn't run 95 percent of their companies—and probably only two or three of the hundreds of members we have could have helped build 1-800-GOT-JUNK? like I did with Brian.

Brian and I were two in a box. We fit together perfectly. The CEOs calling out for a "Cameron" at that conference were desperately hoping there was a quick way to achieve something like that for themselves—but that kind of match is rare.

When I meet CEOs with their COOs, you'd be surprised how often I can see right away that they don't quite fit. And, in other cases, why they fit so perfectly.

Keep reading, and you'll get all my secrets.

THE CHIEF OPERATING OFFICER

A "Cameron" can't be shorthand for a second-in-command. There's no one definition of a COO. Ask yourself this: what does a COO do? Or, more specifically: what do you want your COO to do? I'm going to show you exactly how to know what you're looking for in your COO.

I guarantee that your answer won't be the same as mine. It won't be the same as anyone else's. There are as many ideas about what a COO does or how they do it as there are CEOs. COO is the hardest senior job description to write in any organization. That's why there are magazines and mastermind groups for CEOs, HR executives, heads of marketing and accounting—but there are none for COOs.

There should be—which is why I've created the COO Alliance, which is a network of members from more than seventeen countries where COOs support one another and gain tools and connections to grow themselves and their business.

Just because COO is difficult to define doesn't mean it can't *be* defined. Just because they have hugely varied roles and personalities doesn't mean COOs don't have things in common. For one, they all have to work with a CEO. They're all executing someone else's vision. And they're all in high demand in a business environment dominated by founders and entrepreneurs who are often long on vision and short on execution.

I've interviewed more than 250 COOs for my *Second in Command* podcast. From that experience and running the COO Alliance, I've learned that although COOs come in all shapes and sizes, they fit into broad types. They have different backgrounds and skill sets, though they lean practical rather than visionary. They fill different roles in a company, though they tend toward execution.

I've also been a COO or second-in-command three times. Before I helped build 1-800-GOT-JUNK?, my first second-in-command-type role was with College Pro Painters, the largest residential house painting company on the planet. I then became second-in-command for the franchising company of Boyd Autobody & Glass in Canada, which later acquired Gerber Auto Collision in the US; combined, they are now a $2 billion company. When I started, we had seven locations; when I left, just as the company was about to go public and begin its acquisitions in the United States, we had about sixty. I was also president of a private currency company, Barter

Business Exchange in Vancouver, which was later acquired by UBarter.com, where I became VP of Corporate Development. All that before becoming COO for 1-800-GOT-JUNK?.

So, I know what I'm talking about.

The same COO position in a company can actually have different responsibilities and job descriptions at different times. As we'll see in the first chapter, a famous study in the *Harvard Business Review* identified seven broad types of COOs. I think Brian initially hired me as what the study called a mentor. He wanted to grow the business via franchising but didn't know what he needed to do to achieve that. I did, so I showed him as I was doing it. I later became more like what the study calls "the other half," meaning a foil who complemented Brian's style, knowledge base, and way of working. And 1-800-GOT-JUNK? went on to become a Harvard Business School case study.

Later in the book, we'll see examples of the many different types of COOs and the roles they play, and we'll discuss how you can tell which is the right type for you—and when you need to hire them and where you need to start looking. I'll tell you how best to attract the right person and onboard them effectively. And I'll tell you how to work with them for maximum results in your company, too.

ADAPT OR DIE

The shockwave the COVID-19 pandemic sent through the business world continues to reverberate. Supply chains faltered, and employees quit their jobs in droves in the Great

Resignation (aka Great Realignment, Great Reassessment, etc.). That put even more emphasis on particular skills in any business: strategic thinking, removing obstacles, aligning people, and executing with consistency.

Those responsibilities all typically fall within the role of a COO—making a second-in- command more essential than ever for most entrepreneurs.

A good COO, for example, can help you turn the Great Resignation into a positive force. It's about time employees quit shitty jobs at shitty companies where they have to drive forty minutes each way for the privilege of being treated poorly or working in uninspiring roles. Who wouldn't decide to have a better life if they had the choice? Companies need to build better cultures to attract talent; otherwise, they're dead. The stakes are higher now than they've ever been—and a COO is a CEO's ideal collaborator to get that work done successfully.

There's an old saying that if the rate of change outside your business is greater than the rate of change inside your business, you're out of business. In a full-employment market, it's the same if you're not building a better company. If you've reached the point where you can no longer keep up with the rate of change on your own, the right COO won't just help you stay in the game.

They'll help you positively thrive.

PART 1

COOS: A USER'S GUIDE

CHAPTER 1

WHAT IS A COO?

"Ask questions about everything. If we don't ask questions, we hold ourselves back, and therefore our companies are held back in an unnecessary way. If we have the curiosity and the humility to ask questions and admit when we don't know, we're all so much better off for it."

—BRITTANY CLAUDIUS, FORMER COO ALLIANCE MEMBER AND COO OF SCRIBE MEDIA

When a CEO decides it's time to get help in the business, they may well feel overwhelmed and a little desperate. They're tempted to reach out to the first person who comes along. That's completely the wrong approach. It's unlikely to succeed—and it might well make things worse.

Many of the leadership roles in a business are a little cookie cutter. Most CMOs could be a CMO for most companies; most CFOs could, too. Not the COO. There are COOs who are marketing or franchising ninjas. There are COOs who would fall on their face at both but are fantastic at finance. As Harley

Finkelstein, COO of Shopify, told me on our *Second in Command* podcast, "No two COOs on the planet have the same job."

That's why, as we'll see, the search for a kick-ass COO doesn't start with the COO. It starts with the personality of the CEO, what they need, and the perfect match for their skills and character.

A COO could be outward-facing with a focus on marketing or PR and sales. They could be inward-facing and focus on operations, execution, and engineering. They could be IT-centric. There's only one key requirement, and it's this:

The COO has to be great at whatever the CEO sucks at. Again, it's yin and yang.

At 1-800-GOT-JUNK?, I ran everything except IT and finance. I didn't understand IT, and I didn't like finance. I have a type of dyslexia where I flip all my numbers around, so looking at spreadsheets leaves me a frustrated wreck. But I'm truly world-class at everything related to operations, execution, culture, PR, marketing, sales, branding, people, recruiting, interviewing, selection, onboarding, and training. And that was exactly what Brian needed at the time—especially when I also really knew franchising in the home services space.

He could read the spreadsheets himself.

THE SEVEN TYPES OF COOS

Nate Bennett and Stephen A. Miles wrote a great book on COOs—*Riding Shotgun*—and also a widely read *Harvard*

Business Review article titled "Second in Command: The Misunderstood Role of the Chief Operating Officer." They describe the COO's role as "at once so critical and so situational." They go on: "While other jobs are primarily defined in relation to the work to be done and the structure of the organization, the COO's role is defined in relation to the CEO as an individual."

After interviewing dozens of CEOs and COOs, Bennett and Miles arrived at seven main categories of COO, depending on the role the CEO needs the COO to fill: Executor, Change Agent, Mentor, Other Half, Partner, Heir Apparent, and MVP (of course, a COO can belong to more than one category at the same time, or evolve over time).

EXECUTOR

Perhaps the most traditional COO role is the executor. Traditionally, the executor was needed in operationally intensive industries like airlines and large tech firms, where it would be impossible for the CEO to manage all areas of operations. This second-in- command helps get the work done on a shorter time horizon—daily and quarterly—while the CEO sets the longer-term vision. The executor is maybe what most people think of when they hear the title COO: the classic behind-the-scenes collaborator who "makes it so."

A CEO puts an executor in place to get shit done. When I wrote my first book, *Double Double*, its working title was *How to Get More Shit Done with Less People, Faster*. Well, that's the role of the executor—you transfer your ideas and information to them, and they execute the things you want to happen. (And it's true to say that execution in some form or another represents a core role for all seconds in command.)

CHANGE AGENT

The change agent comes in to oversee a major company turnaround or even a massive growth phase. To that extent, they're a little like a crisis consultant, but usually the process requires more work and oversight over a longer time horizon. Perhaps the company is in financial peril, struggling to stay ahead of competitors, or moving in a new direction. One example is Larry Ellison hiring Ray Lane from Booz Allen Hamilton to turn around sales and marketing at Oracle. Change agents can drive transformation and handle the blowback when an organization needs to shake up business as usual to survive or level up.

A change agent usually comes from the outside because that makes it easier for them to see the business differently and to bring a fresh perspective to the problems as well as potential solutions—though their precise scope and tenure will depend on what needs to change. A change-agent COO might coordinate making a complete pivot in the organization, such as entering a new sector; transitioning from in-person to virtual work; taking a US-based company global; or they might oversee major mergers and acquisitions.

Change agents help effect transformation when the team won't listen to the CEO or leaders inside the organization. This is when changing a company culture is like dealing with teenagers. I thought some of my friends' parents were far more amazing than mine, so there was a much greater chance of me listening to them than to my own mom and dad.

My friends, of course, were more likely to listen to my folks than to their own.

Sometimes, people are more open to learning from those they know least. I coached Ben Kirschner, CEO of EliteSEM (now called Tinuiti), and his COO, Zach Morrison (now CEO of Tinuiti), for four years, and their team called me "Uncle Cameron" because they listened to my advice like they would have their own uncle's.

MENTOR

A mentor COO commonly comes into a business to support a CEO such as a young founder in a startup that scales too rapidly for the CEO's managerial ability to keep up. Bennett and Miles give the example of Mort Topfer, who was in his fifties in 1994 when he was brought in to serve as COO to twenty-nine-year-old Michael Dell. For a founder CEO to accept this kind of support, however, they must have a certain level of self-awareness and maturity. Above all, they have to be willing to admit what they don't know.

When I first started at 1-800-GOT-JUNK?, I played a mentor role to Brian, who needed to franchise but recognized he didn't have the knowledge base or skill set to do so on his own. I helped him with franchise manuals, franchise training, franchise coaching, marketing plans, budgets, building teams for all department areas, and other issues he didn't even know he didn't know. I'd already grown two franchise companies. He trusted me, *and* I had the skills he didn't have.

I actually started as a coach to Brian's VP of Operations, but that VP Operations walked into Brian's office within two weeks and said, "I can't do anything Cameron is trying to teach me. I'll never be able to learn what he does. We just need to bring him on board." As a mentor, I knew what we had to do, and I could go in and do it. The team members called me "uncle," because I was older than everybody else in the company at the time. I was even the first executive to have kids.

The COO often serves as a mentor to a young or inexperienced CEO, as Sheryl Sandberg did for Mark Zuckerberg at Facebook. She came in when Facebook was a very small company, only operating on university campuses, and mentored a twenty-three-year-old kid who had never built a business before.

Many tech founders are young and don't have the depth of understanding to build and scale a company. They understand the tech and how to offer a solution, but they need help with the business side. That's why mentor COOs have become so common in the tech space over the past decade or so.

(By the way, if you're in the tech space, I'd suggest hiring a COO who has experience in and understanding of your exact industry. There are other niches where it also makes sense to have domain expertise—engineering-related areas, or the automotive industry, say—but in others like home services, it's far less important.)

OTHER HALF

For me, every COO is to some degree or other an "other half." It's one of my central beliefs that you can only leverage the power of two by making the relationship between CEO and COO like a marriage. Any COO has to serve as the yin to your yang (or vice versa). It's the quintessential "two in a box" configuration. And just as every CEO has their own personality type, strengths, areas of expertise, weaknesses, needs, demands, working methods, foibles, doubts, and anxieties, so every CEO has a few possible COOs—maybe just one perfect COO—who will provide a balancing role in virtually every aspect. Who's up at thirty thousand feet when the CEO is down in the weeds, or deep in the day-to-day when the CEO is strategically thinking two years out, or making sure sales literature is printed and ready for distribution while the CEO is on TV selling their vision.

It makes sense for an outward-facing CEO with a big personality to have a more technical, inward-facing COO. Or for an inward-facing CEO to bring in a COO to do the public-facing stuff the CEO thinks is a waste of time.

As I say, every COO has to be at least partly an other half. Once I had helped Brian build a franchise infrastructure at 1-800-GOT-JUNK?, that's what happened to me. I love public speaking and motivating people, which complemented Brian's natural strengths, so I became his other half.

Finding your other half is not easy—just as no one achieves a perfect marriage without putting time, effort, and emotion into dating—but it's worth the effort, particularly if you're a strong, solid, seasoned CEO but you recognize you have areas of weakness; a COO who fills in those gaps will help leverage you, and your firm, to the next level.

PARTNER

In many ways, I see the partner as a variation on the "other half." It's when a CEO chooses to co-lead and puts the COO right in the same box with them on the org chart. A partner might bring other skill sets to the table you don't have, but they could also simply free up your time by taking enough work off your plate to enable you to stop working 100-hour weeks and get your life back. Not every CEO thrives in a co-leadership arrangement—because lines and responsibilities can be blurred, and toes can get stepped on—but those who do find that it can hugely leverage their ability and encourage their ambitions. The partner COO may even be a co-founder and co-investor in the company, but they clearly are not the visionary part of the partnership.

HEIR APPARENT

If you're looking for a successor, the COO role can be a way to identify and cultivate an heir apparent. It gives a COO a chance to learn all aspects of the business, while also giving the CEO the opportunity to ensure the potential successor has the right leadership qualities before handing over the reins. The key thing about an "heir apparent" COO is that their succession is not guaranteed. We're not talking about the British throne, where everyone knows the line of succession. Heir apparent is a chance for a COO to prove themselves and for a CEO to see them at work. Sometimes things go wrong; the COO turns out not to be the best fit for future CEO and goes their own way, while the CEO continues to look for a successor. However, effective COO to CEO transitions under this model include two generations of CEOs at Continental Airlines, Gordon Bethune and Larry Kellner; and Jevon

McCormick, who took over leadership of Scribe Media from founders Tucker Max and Zach Obront after originally starting as their COO.

When it works, using the COO role to groom an heir apparent helps ensure a succession plan. One member of the COO Alliance, Matt Wool, moved from COO to President when his CEO moved into the chairman role of Acceleration Partners. Zach Morrison (one of my coaching clients and a founding COO Alliance member), President and CEO of Tinuiti, ranked number two by Glassdoor, was previously COO. He was groomed as heir apparent when the CEO was preparing to exit to Chairman.

The heir apparent is usually an internal hire, but they could also be someone from the outside with deep domain expertise and a proven leadership record.

MVP

The final type of COO identified in the *HBR* article is the MVP. This is a special case that occurs when an internal lead is so integral to the operation of the company that a CEO promotes them to COO to avoid losing them to a competitor. That promotion comes with the respect of the whole team. Such a COO may grow into an heir apparent, but from the CEO's point of view the strategy focuses on recognizing achievement through internal promotion, thus driving retention.

My COO title at 1-800-GOT-JUNK? partly came from my MVP status. I originally joined as a coach to one of Brian's executives and then became VP of Operations. After I had contributed significantly to the company, one of the other VPs said in a leadership meeting, "Cameron really is COO. He knows what he's doing. He's running this place...Why don't we just give him the damn title?"

MVP roles develop when you identify an emerging leader in a similar situation. Some CEOs create the position when they recognize that a leader has stepped up within the company and is handling operations better than they were. When I became Brian's COO, eventually franchise sales reported to me, the call center reported to me, and I even co-led board meetings. I was better at some aspects of the business than Brian, and he was happy to hand off those responsibilities.

An MVP is critical because they are doing work *no one* else in the organization can do. Promoting them to COO can elevate the brand to another level. One of the first people I interviewed for the *Second in Command* podcast, Harley Finkelstein at Shopify, is a perfect example. The CEO didn't want to lose him, because Harvey focuses on business development and is an outward face. He rose to COO even before he had the experience for the job, mainly because he embodied the right perception of the company.

ROLES OF THE COO

The seven main categories are a useful framework for assessing what type of COO you need—or already have. But the roles the COO plays blur into one another: Adult in the Room; Follower v. Devil's Advocate; Design and Execution; Integrator; and Moderator and Enforcer. COOs can move from one type to another or be more than one type at the same time. Ultimately, again, there are as many different COOs as there are CEOs, but there are certain common roles CEOs most often need a COO to play.

ADULT IN THE ROOM

In recent decades, a big role of the COO has been to be the adult in the room. This is particularly true for the emerging tech business run by a younger technical founder who needs some supervision. There's some truth in the stereotype of tech founders as technical geniuses in headphones tapping away at their keyboards in the dark without the ability to build relationships, hire the right people, do marketing, sales, and HR, or even know whether the business is doing well. In this scenario, a COO tends to run the company around the CEO's technical expertise—and helps interpret the business world for the CEO.

Now that technical expertise is more widespread and better understood, other people are doing the programming, and most tech CEOs have better-rounded business skills. Businesspeople across the board understand technology better, and many technical founders now have the aptitude to continue to scale. Today, COOs in those businesses are less of an adult in the room and more of a partner in the adventure.

The dynamic within startups has changed as the breadth of technology has spread across all business areas. Twenty years ago, only tech geeks understood technology: it was a programming rabbit hole whose inhabitants didn't understand anything about business. Now, everyone knows what a server is, what programmers do...and that a whole ecosystem has grown up that allows you to outsource any kind of technical work to people who understand it. It's no longer unusual for a founder to build a company that involves technology without necessarily knowing how to code; and some of the largest companies are tech-based, from social media platforms to e-commerce.

In *High Growth Handbook,* author Elad Gil describes how many startups scale by having the technical founders focus on the product while they bring in an ops person to help them scale it: the COO. Gad discusses how the COO can build out the executive team and take on areas the founders don't have time for, are poorly suited to, or don't want to focus on.

While the COO takes strategic execution pieces off the CEO's desk, they need to be careful not just to become a dumping ground for every other business area apart from the CEO's own projects. Their role is to help the other business areas grow their skills and confidence by delegating action to business area heads.

Being a startup or scaling COO is not about *doing* stuff; it's about *getting stuff done.*

FOLLOWER VS. DEVIL'S ADVOCATE

Some CEOs need a COO who will simply execute what they tell them. Others benefit more from being challenged. These COOs are what I call, respectively, the follower and the devil's advocate. A follower COO takes the CEO's vision and makes it happen—because the CEO doesn't know how to, can't, or doesn't want to. This role works well in smaller companies with entrepreneurial CEOs who are happy to delegate much of what needs to get done. The CEO and the COO are like partners: to put it simply, they are the thinker and the doer.

The role of the devil's advocate COO is completely different. They often come in from outside a business to challenge the status quo, serve as a change agent, and to deliberately challenge the CEO to stop doing things the way they've always been done. Maybe they're experts in scaling or automation, or maybe their background in other fields gives them innovative or disruptive ideas. They're there to question a CEO's biases and ideas, perhaps when a business needs a restart after decades of operating in a particular way.

A devil's advocate causes upheaval. For that reason, they have to combine their ideas with outstanding people skills and an ability to defuse conflict. They need to be able to build consensus by challenging the CEO's ideas rather than simply disrupting the company and board through constant arguing for its own sake.

Unhealthy debate doesn't serve anyone—or the business.

DESIGN AND EXECUTION

Even with a devil's advocate COO, the basic relationship with the CEO remains the same. The CEO defines the vision of the organization, and the COO helps to figure out how to make that vision come true, either by following or by challenging. The CEO defines what the culture looks and feels like, and the COO figures out how to make it happen.

The CEO is like a homeowner, and the COO is like a general contractor. The homeowner decides what home they want built, and the contractor figures out how to build it. No homeowner would ask a contractor, "What would you like this home to look like?" The contractor might say, "The doorway would work better if it were over there rather than here," or "This would be cheaper in wood than in metal," and their ideas might be great—but the tail should never wag the dog.

By the same token, the homeowner shouldn't try to explain to a contractor how to wire electrical, pull plumbing, or pour a foundation. That's the contractor's job. The CEO describes the what—and then leaves the COO to figure out the how and the who to make it happen.

INTEGRATOR

The role of the COO is partly shaped by the size of a business.

In very small businesses, the second-in-command is often more of a right hand to the CEO rather than a true COO. A startup might aspire to get big enough to need a COO but not get there for a while. When the CEO gets to a point where they realize they can't do it all or don't know how to do it all, they need a partner or mentor to assist them. The first second-in-command is often an MVP from within the business.

When a company gets to the position of hiring its first COO, it is often the first true seasoned, senior role. In this case, the new COO will represent a major hire who will bring substantive change throughout the company. Author Gino Wickman, who wrote a couple of books that talked about the second-in-command role—*Rocket Fuel* and *Traction*—sees this type of

COO as an integrator for the CEO and the CEO's vision into the company.

In this view, the CEO is a visionary who should focus on the core areas of culture, vision, and direction. They generate lots of ideas without necessarily knowing how to execute. In smaller companies in particular, visionary CEOs also have trouble staying focused. They pursue too many ideas at once, creating whiplash inside the organization, and struggle to develop their leaders and managers. They're geniuses with a thousand helpers, so they need a second-in-command to introduce standardized systems and procedures to facilitate clarity, communication, and accountability.

When a CEO struggles with the people side of the business or plateaus in profit generation, it may be time to bring in an integrator COO who can help prioritize the random swirl of projects, adhere to a budget, and ensure follow-through.

Wickman describes the role of the integrator like this:

An Integrator is the person who is the tiebreaker for the leadership team, is the glue for the organization, holds everything together, beats the drum (provides cadence), is accountable for the P&L results, executes the business plan, holds the Leadership Team accountable, and is the steady force in the organization. The Integrator also creates organizational clarity, communication, and consistency; typically (but not always) operates more on logic; drives results; forces resolution, focus, team unity, prioritization, and follow-through; is the filter for all of the Visionary's ideas; harmoniously integrates the Leadership Team; and helps to remove obstacles and barriers.

This kind of model works well in smaller companies—say fifty employees or fewer, or perhaps $1 million to $15 million—and some parts of the role, such as being accountable for P&L results and executing the business plan, are relevant whatever the size of the company. But in larger companies with many more teams and moving parts, the concept of integration becomes far more complex.

Take my story at 1-800-GOT-JUNK?, where we doubled revenue each year, growing from $2 million to $106 million, with three thousand employees. It was lightning growth, but by that point, I was tearing my hair out. The company felt huge. Then Launi Skinner, the former President of Starbucks USA, came on board as COO and said, "What a cute little company."

We had a very different frame of reference. At its new size, the company needed a new type of COO.

MODERATOR AND ENFORCER

The visionary–integrator model also risks the CEO-visionary abdicating too much responsibility. As a leadership team starts to scale, decisions might require a tiebreaker—but it should be the CEO. It doesn't make business sense for a CEO to vest tiebreaking decisions in a COO. Instead, the COO should be the person who enables *real* discussion to take place in the organization by getting people to say what they mean to avoid miscommunication and passive-aggression. They don't take sides; instead, they build collaboration and consensus so the team can solve their own problems, get on the same page, and be their own tiebreaker.

The COO serves as a moderator who gets all the other business areas working well together. They should be building a harmonious leadership team and organizing subject-matter experts to collaborate, build consensus, have healthy debates, and be in alignment. If the alignment doesn't exist, the decisions can't be made.

In smaller companies without accountable management teams, a COO might need to enforce accountability, but not in a larger company. As a company scales to medium or enterprise level, the leadership team should be able to hold themselves accountable. Rather than holding people accountable, the COO hires *accountable people*.

As we've seen, the contrast Wickman draws between a logical COO and an entrepreneurial CEO who is a scattered idea-generation machine is a little out of date now. More and more businesses are growing and becoming professionally managed over time as the CEO grows and learns. There are far fewer scattered CEOs, generally. And many top CEOs and entrepreneurs invest in their own leadership growth by participating in mastermind groups like YPO, EO, Genius Network, Strategic Coach, WarRoom, Mastermind Talks, Baby Bathwater, etc. The trend of CEOs growing their own skills with groups like these and with coaching has started to finally trickle down to them getting their senior leadership into coaching arrangements, mentorships, and mastermind groups like the COO Alliance, as well.

Wickman sees the role of the COO to serve as the glue in an organization. I see it slightly differently. I see *culture* as the glue that holds the organization together, and the CEO and COO as the source of that culture—through their vision, obsession with core values, and motivation toward goals. Collective alignment promotes cohesion, rather than a single individual.

It's not just me who sees things differently from Wickman. Zach Morrison of Tinuiti agrees that there may not be such a clear dichotomy between visionary and integrator, saying: "Over time, the COO needs to be both, and the CEO becomes the coach on both vs. *the* visionary."

CHAPTER 2

WHAT'S THE POINT OF A COO?

"A COO makes things happen! They are the glue that holds all internal departments and processes together. COOs take a CEO's vision and find a way to make it a reality."

—ALAN JOSKOWICZ, COO ALLIANCE MEMBER
AND COO OF DYNAMIC MARKETING, INC.

We've seen that a COO can occupy a variety of spaces and serve a range of functions. There is no single template for what makes an effective COO, other than their fit with the CEO—and every CEO is different.

Take it from me. Through the COO Alliance and my *Second in Command* podcast, I've come into contact with hundreds of COOs with a wide range of skill sets in a wide variety of businesses. No matter how strong they are in their particular role, they all have one thing in common: they would likely do a terrible job running 90 percent of other companies. Of more than 250 podcast guests, each might be suitable to run, say, twenty of the other companies represented—and completely unsuitable to run the rest.

The most requested guest to have on the *Second in Command* podcast is Sheryl Sandberg, who was COO of FaceBook for fifteen years. Everyone wants to learn from her, and to learn about the incredibly powerful relationship she built with CEO and founder Mark Zuckerberg. There's no guarantee things would have gone so well with a different COO.

That's not to say that COOs don't have certain things in common. Good COOs have the ability to slow down, think strategically, grow and align people, and focus on the critical few things rather than the important many. The true power of two in a box comes when the COO matches those traits with the unique personality of the CEO, and sometimes also with industry-specific expertise.

You might still be wondering, what can a COO do for me? The answer's pretty simple: they can do anything you want them to. You just need to know what that is and select your second-in-command accordingly.

INWARD- VS. OUTWARD-FACING

Some CEOs are so outward-facing they become integrally tied to the marketing and brand, as Steve Jobs did at Apple, or Elon Musk at Tesla. The general public is almost as familiar with the CEO's name as with the product. In those cases, the right COO is likely more inward-facing and focused on the behind-the-scenes operations. There's no reason for them ever to become known to the public. Who could name the COO of Samsung off the top of their head?

In contrast, other CEOs are inward-facing. They're like the "Level 5" leaders Jim Collins describes in *Good to Great*: humble, driven, and focused, a combination that allows them to be inspirations for their colleagues. Rather than engaging with marketing and branding, they might specialize in engineering or finance and lack any desire to engage with the media. This type of CEO can build a highly recognized brand without their name becoming widely known. In such a situation, a public-facing COO would make sense, to serve as the face of the company in the media and as a spokesperson in the business world.

Ben & Jerry's provides a great example of an outward-facing COO. The ice cream maker is run by Ben Cohen and Jerry Greenfield, respectively inward- and outward-facing. Their powerful yin and yang has helped build and project a brand that's recognized around the world.

At Shopify, Harley Finkelstein, who went from COO to President, is the face of marketing, does many of the media interviews, and runs business development. CEO Tobias Lütke is inward-facing, spending his time on product engineering and finance.

At 1-800-GOT-JUNK?, I was a highly outward-facing COO focused on franchise sales, marketing, talking to the press, and doing speaking events. I was part of the amplification of the message and the brand, which leveraged my gifts and was appropriate for the growth phase, which brought with it a lot of built-in PR. As I explained in my book *Free PR*, I understood how publicity worked. That's not always the skill of a COO, but it was highly useful at that phase of the business growth. Brian and I became a public duo. We'd sometimes give speaking events in which we took turns through a whole talk, being on stage at the same time.

By contrast, Erik Church has now held my former role for a decade, and most people have never heard of him. He built the company from $100 million to $400 million, but he doesn't do speaking events on behalf of the brand or engage on social media. He's inward-focused, operational...and fantastic at what he does.

The key, again, is that the COO serves as the CEO's counterpart, whether that means being in the backroom or facing the media. It's similar to two spouses going to a cocktail party, with one an extrovert and one more introverted. They both have amazing discussions, but they approach socializing differently, and they're more effective together than individually.

While it's highly unusual for the COO to be the external face of the company beyond playing a role in marketing and communications, they are almost always the internal face of the company and the top-level manager on the org chart. More often than not, the CEO will either have very few or no direct reports, or only the COO will report to them.

Once you hire a COO, you don't need to supervise more leaders than him or her if you don't want to.

COORDINATION VS. SUBJECT-MATTER EXPERTISE

COO Alliance member Rachel Pachivas, of Annmarie Skin Care, likens the COO role to being a quarterback. All she does is call the plays and pass the ball—and trust that everyone else is fulfilling their own roles.

The COO can't do everything, and hiring a new second-in-command isn't going to replace subject-matter expertise. A COO might focus on finance, IT, sales and marketing, operations, or business areas, but as the company scales, those areas still need their own heads. The exact configuration depends on individual bandwidth and the maturity of the company. A COO leading seven business areas can be an outstanding marketer—but they'll likely still need to appoint a head of marketing, too.

Subject-matter expertise is less important in a COO than an adaptable personality and the ability to talk to department areas and call the plays without sounding like a moron. Department heads have to be experts, but they don't have to understand others. COOs have to be chameleons who understand everyone. They don't have to be experts; they just need to know how to *hire* experts.

The Head of IT is likely the smartest person in IT, and the CFO is likely the smartest person in finance. The only disciplines the COO is likely the smartest person in are communications, people skills, and leadership. They need the competence to ask the right questions from a leadership perspective: which systems are missing or broken, and how can the company change to collaborate better or to remove obstacles?

The COO can lean on the Socratic method. They need enough business savvy to know what questions to ask, to get the right answers, to work with their people, and to bring out the best in others by growing their skills and confidence. All of that involves removing obstacles between business areas, aligning those business areas, fixing the areas that are broken, and bringing out the best in each one by adding the right systems, people, and resources.

The COO must be able to speak many different languages—but doesn't have to be fluent in any of them. When I oversaw product development at 1-800-GOT-JUNK?, I would talk to the IT team about what software they needed to build. It didn't matter that I understood shit of what they said most of the time, as long as I grasped enough to ask the right questions. The same with finance. Figures are not my inherent strength, though I still had to understand the P&L, budgets, and cash flow statements. But not so much the balance sheet.

A COO must understand how every department speaks and translate between them. That's how they ensure alignment, collaboration, and necessary cross-departmental discussions in advance of taking action. The COO is part matchmaker and part cheerleader, and ensures people in different departments have the necessary facts about what others are doing.

It's a balance. The COO needs results, but they also have to be able to listen and build confidence. If they're saying no to suggestions, and making all decisions themselves, they're not building the confidence of their team to make decisions, come up with the right answers, and develop competency and skill. No one can develop if they're not allowed to do anything for themselves.

EMPOWERMENT, NOT RESCUE

The COO's job is not to fix the problems or answer all the questions, but rather to grow others so *they* can fix the problems and *they* can answer the questions. By focusing on growing people instead of fixing problems directly, the COO can advance the organization strategically rather than becoming just another firefighter.

The purpose of a COO taking work from a swamped CEO is not simply to have a swamped COO.

One of my favorite comparisons is with the role of a parent. A parent's job is not to cook every meal or do all the laundry for their children, but rather to teach them how to do those tasks for themselves, so they have self-sufficiency when they reach adulthood. In the same way, a good COO hovers above the trenches and helps coordinate what's happening down there rather than getting sucked into the mud by trying to do employees' work for them. Growing others' skills, competence, and confidence is a much more effective long-term strategy. (I could go on here about giving someone a fish and teaching them how to fish, but you get the point.)

I've spoken to many COOs on the *Second in Command* podcast about how they oversee so many areas, and they essentially all say the same thing: they don't. They don't even try to be on top of everything everyone else is doing. Their role is to grow and align people who will oversee different areas and improve collaboration between them.

A COO who gets involved in every decision for every business area will soon be overwhelmed. They'll be incapacitated. It's impossible for one person even to read enough emails to keep on top of every business area, let alone make any decisions.

But that's not their job. Their job is to lead people to do rather than doing directly.

Another role of the COO is to be able to find the greatest point of leverage in a messy situation. At one point at 1-800-GOT-JUNK?, the Head of Product Development was working with the Head of IT. They fought constantly, with lots of cross-cultural issues and a large dollop of misogyny thrown in. Communication finally broke down completely when one said to the other, "You're just like my mother."

Yep, that would do it.

I had to swoop in to help teach them how to communicate effectively, but I made damn sure I didn't take over any work from either of them. They had to learn to disagree but still collaborate and have a basic level of respect and affinity for one another. I was a coach, not a substitute worker.

It's easy sometimes to forget that the COO isn't just an execution expert. They're also a people expert. All COOs possess this unique skill set: processes and people, the nuts and bolts of getting shit done combined with EQ and soft skills that most shitkickers don't begin to understand.

SYSTEMS AND SHORTCUTS

Because the COO is an execution expert, they need to understand systems. A good COO—particularly someone from outside a business—can see shortcuts, embrace the new, have the ability to learn quickly, and figure out how to hack the system.

Seeing shortcuts was one of my strengths because I found it easy to dumb everything down to the lowest common denominator. Momentum creates momentum, so I always saw my role as being about getting things done rather than making them perfect. That way, we could move on to the next thing. I had to find the easiest ways to get work done, because we couldn't have the smartest, most senior people working on every project. COOs have to be quick thinkers who can read between the lines to signpost potential snags in the underlying systems.

One of my mentors, Gregg Johnson, tells a story about when he was being groomed as the COO and senior exec at Starbucks. The CEO called him one day about a sign at a Starbucks location in Seattle with a burned out letter "B."

The CEO didn't ask Gregg why the letter wasn't working. He didn't care, because that wasn't a leadership question. The key question, and the one the CEO asked Greg, was what system could be put in place to ensure that every letter on every sign at all fourteen thousand Starbucks locations was always working.

A good COO knows the value of the old business saying by Michael Gerber, who wrote *The E-Myth*: "People don't fail—systems fail."

The CEO needs to be able to rely on the COO to keep their eye on the leadership questions without being distracted. It's made easier if the COO can identify broken or missing systems and create a no-blame environment in which people feel they are allowed to fail, as long as they stay focused on the systemic solution.

A COO can also complement the CEO's vision by looking beyond the business to the environment in which it operates: the customer, the supplier, the market, the economy. They look at the horizon and try to predict what lies beyond—and they feed that information into the company strategy.

At one point at 1-800-GOT-JUNK?, the Canadian dollar was at about 62 cents to the US dollar. I went to the team and said I was worried about the Canadian dollar getting stronger. They didn't see a problem. Six months later, it was at seventy cents to the US dollar. I said I was worried about it going to par. A year later, it reached seventy-eight cents, and people started listening to me. We implemented forward-rate contracts and hedging strategies. Eventually, the Canadian dollar surpassed the US dollar and was worth $1.07.

We would have lost a hundred thousand dollars each year for every penny it went up had I not been keeping an eye on macroeconomic forces. Macroeconomics wasn't my "job." It wasn't part of my brief. But it *was* part of my brief to think about finance, operations, and the customers in the market. That was the sort of integration I could bring to the table as the COO.

Strategy and people go closely together. It's only by understanding people that a COO can fix strategy and find shortcuts. Take the franchise model. There are obviously different levels of franchise partners. Some have a background in management consulting or running businesses, while others have nothing like that business competency. But they all need to be able to execute the business system. The same goes for internal employees.

My goal was to put systems in place that I could write on a Post-It note so that the worst employee in the worst market in the worst conditions could still execute them. If a franchisee could follow a system in Buffalo, in a snowstorm in February, with a temporary employee, then I knew we had the right system.

Anything that required an MBA to figure out was too complicated.

Complicated is easy; simple is hard. Insiders don't necessarily look for or see shortcuts, which is why CEOs find that hiring a COO from outside can bring a different perspective to the table. I was never the smartest person in the room—unless the room was very small—but from school onward I was always the student who figured out the shortcuts. I found the cheat sheets, I borrowed lecture notes, I paid smart kids to do assignments. I got the information I needed as efficiently as I could.

COOs need the same perspective on business systems: they need an integrated, efficiency-minded, and scalable vision. They need to know when there might be an easier way to achieve the same goal.

They need constructive laziness.

STRATEGY VS. TACTICS

Around 2,500 years ago, the Chinese general and military genius Sun Tzu, wrote *The Art of War*. In it, he said: "Strategy without tactics is the slowest route to victory. Tactics without strategy is the noise before defeat."

In other words, you need them both.

In business, strategy and tactics should always complement each other. They're two sides of the same coin. In broad terms, the CEO is in charge of strategy, and the COO is in charge of tactics. Both are useless without the other.

One of the overriding goals of the COO is to provide high-level support to the CEO. That doesn't mean that lower-level tasks are always a waste of time; but, like the CEO, the COO needs to keep a strategic view on culture, the direction of the board, and risk management. For an entrepreneurial CEO who hires a COO as a first leadership team member, especially, the COO can be a partner to brainstorm with at a time when the CEO is likely crying out for strategic advice.

That also frees up other leaders to stay relatively focused on their business areas and get tactical. And the COO can also periodically drop into the day-to-day execution of different business areas without becoming consumed or losing sight of the strategic level.

If that makes COO sound like something of a bipolar role, that's because it is. Strategy on one hand, day-to-day operations on the other. It's the COO's job to toggle between head up and head down. They need to make sure they're on the same page with your Vivid Vision, then check how that strategy is being translated into the operational level, and then check back in with the high level to see if anything has changed.

It's like a whale coming up for air and then diving back down to feed.

Harley Finkelstein, of Shopify, describes the role like this: "As a COO, make sure that you continuously recalibrate your role, your responsibilities, and your area of focus with your CEO. Just because your CEO told you, 'Here's what you should do,' it doesn't mean he or she hasn't changed their mind."

As a CEO, it's key to allow the COO to move between those levels. They shouldn't be put into silos or used to put out fires in particular business areas. That's only going to harm strategy. Remember Gregg Johnson's story of the broken Starbucks sign. Why something is broken is a tactical concern. The strategic concern is about what malfunctioning or missing system allowed the sign to *become* broken. If the CEO doesn't allow the COO to occupy the same strategic level, they'll end up pushing them down to the tactical level.

And that will destroy the leverage that comes from two-in-a-box.

As CEO, you look outward, work with VCs, raise money, and so on. You climb the mountain to see where the organization is going, and the COO makes sure you get there. But they can't do that unless you take them up the mountain with you and let them share the view.

SELF-AWARENESS AND PERSONALITY

One of the most powerful roles a COO can play in any company is as a source of energy. Their energy creates more energy—but they have to appreciate their own power. If they bring excitement and optimism, those qualities will spread. If they come into a company with stressed-out energy, they'll stress out everyone else. A demanding hard-ass will get a response in kind. They shouldn't need to agonize over every word they say (if they do, the CEO has probably hired the wrong person), but they should be thoughtful and have a keen awareness that what they say impacts the whole organization.

More than anyone except the CEO—and sometimes even more than *them*—every action of the COO creates a butterfly effect throughout a whole business.

One of my biggest mistakes as a COO was an incident in which I got upset with my entire team for wasting time in meetings. My point wasn't wrong; shit, we were wasting hour after hour. But I blew up about it, and the effects were even worse than the time-wasting. It spread negative energy throughout the whole company for a month. It would have been better not to say anything. Best of all would have been to explain it in a different way that achieved a better result—and frankly, any result would have been better than what I achieved.

That's a lesson that stuck with me.

EMOTIONAL MATURITY

Whatever qualities a CEO needs from a COO, and whatever role they want them to play in the business, one of the key requirements is emotional maturity. That doesn't emerge overnight, which is why the best fits for the second-in-command role tend to be more seasoned executives who have had the time to gain wisdom and experience. That said, I've met some incredibly impressive younger COOs who have an understanding beyond their years—combining people and technology skills, for example.

Experience can be overrated, and not all experience is created equal. Some people who say they have thirty years' experience actually have five years' experience, six times in a row. There's no reason a twenty-seven-year-old with five years of experience and more technological knowledge couldn't be a better hire.

The key to experience is nothing to do with years; it's to do with the maturity and wisdom that come from having seen situations before, from having hired and fired, built teams, been to board meetings, and whatever else. Everything we've done before makes us better, but some people gain maturity and wisdom quicker.

I'm pretty relaxed when my son sets out to travel across the world on his own at the age of 18 because he's already flown a lot. At that age, I would have found it impossible to do the same; but I trust him far more than I would have trusted my younger self because he has done it all before.

That's the same trust a CEO needs to be able to put in a COO—that they've seen and done enough not to mistake a problem for a disaster, or to see success as the same thing as perfection.

There's no fixed age for being able to do that.

SHAPING CULTURE

The culture of an organization emerges from the core values, core purpose, the Vivid Vision, the big hairy audacious goal (BHAG), the people, and the leadership skills you cultivate in your managers. The CEO decides on the culture of the company based on their Vivid Vision, and the COO helps to make it a reality. The COO can positively steer and cultivate the culture, because the best culture is created by design rather than default.

The COO helps change the culture as needed, based on their knowledge of what you want to build. They could fire five negative, toxic people and change the culture overnight. They could build a culture of praise based on the core values, implement awards, incorporate mantras like "People don't fail—systems fail," and create a positive, no-blame environment. They could apply accountability and goals.

With Brian, I had room to exercise my entrepreneurial mindset in the COO role because the company was very new. I joined as the fourteenth employee. They didn't have all the answers and systems yet, so we had to wing it. There was no franchise training system, coaching system, sales system, marketing plan, marketing budget, or metrics. There was nothing in place; we had to create it all. I had to be entrepreneurial enough to make it up.

COOs in early-stage companies or entrepreneurial businesses often face a similar blank canvas. If systems don't exist, you'll need a COO who can create them—and that's very different from being able to put them into place. Someone who can run a two-hundred-person company isn't necessarily the best

COO to build a company from ten to two hundred people; running a company of a thousand people needs different skills than growing a company from a hundred to a thousand people.

In an entrepreneurial company, make sure to hire a COO with entrepreneurial chops.

WORKING WITH THE BOARD AND CUSTOMERS

The COO also has a role in communicating with the board. They bring operational clarity, a connection between the vision and the tactical discipline that the board appreciates, and often data-based answers that an entrepreneurial CEO doesn't have. They can fill in the rest of the story the CEO leaves out. They also bring the board's questions and concerns back to the leadership team to get the work done, and they hold the business areas to a higher standard by ensuring details don't fall through the cracks.

It's not the role of the COO to reach out to the board between board meetings. As CEO, on the other hand, you can reach out to the board whenever and however you want. The COO should not go directly to the board or any board member, because it will cause triangulation with the CEO, which is dangerous. The COO is a participant, not an initiator.

As COO, I helped craft board meeting agendas and steer the discussion topics. My teams prepared the information the board received in advance. But I never called meetings. I formed a bridge between the board and the execution, while ensuring proper preparation so the CEO didn't gloss over any important areas. The COO's job is to make sure the CEO shows up at the meeting with information that is accurate without being scary.

It goes without saying that the CEO and COO have to be united in front of the board. If you have differences, sort them out before you walk into the boardroom.

It's also great for COOs to be involved directly with customers to get a fuller picture of the business. They should talk to customers, suppliers, and all stakeholders to understand what you're building and what the concerns are. Michael Dell used to call it "reading the tea leaves"—he got a fuller picture by reading all the customer comments. Sadly, too few leaders are truly connected to their customers or suppliers.

DESIRABLE QUALITIES

Identifying the right second-in-command can be a challenge, as there are so few people who will fit a role perfectly. There are, however, some common qualities you should expect any COO to be able to contribute toward an organization.

ADAPTABILITY

The first, not surprisingly, is adaptability. The COO needs to tailor their approach based on the culture of the organization, rather than trying to adapt the culture to suit them. They need to absorb, project, and become the guardian of that culture. They're the keeper of the flame.

TIME MANAGEMENT

There will always be too much for a COO to do, so they need the ability to multitask and exercise excellent time management.

DRIVE

The COO is the motor that drives the whole business forward. They can't afford to rest on their achievements. When 1-800-GOT-JUNK? won an award and was on *Oprah*, I was less interested in the short-term excitement than in how we could use our appearance to get more coverage and ensure the call center was equipped to field the greater influx of inquiries. We were great, sure, but while Brian and the team understandably reveled in the success for a couple of weeks, I made sure to leverage the excitement throughout the company in a way that would make a long-term difference.

LIKEABILITY

No one wants to work with people they don't like, and that's more true of a COO than virtually anyone else. A COO has to be likable as a person, because that will give them a platform to facilitate the whole leadership team and steer the culture of the organization. They need to build consensus within the business, as well as deal with suppliers, customers, and the board. Likeability was one of my core strengths. I stuck to my small-town values from growing up in Northern Ontario in Canada, which made it easier to build relationships with all sorts of people.

HONESTY

Honesty was another of my strengths, because I've always been open and frank. Part of the COO's role, as I saw it, was to say what everybody else was thinking but didn't have the confidence to say. A COO with a filter is of limited help. They should be respectful and discreet, of course, but they shouldn't have to censor their communication. The more guarded they are, the less others will trust them.

Say what you mean and mean what you say. It's not rocket science.

COMMUNICATION

We have all worked with leaders who make us roll our eyes or want to duck out of sight. When the COO walks by, people should feel excited to spend time with them rather than trying to avoid them. That's a key part of the COO bringing drive to the business—and it all comes down to communication.

When I asked COOs what advice they'd give to their twenty-two-year-old selves, Matt Wool, COO Alliance member and President of Acceleration Partners, said: "Listen before you talk, always. It's number one." It's not as simple as being able to communicate well. A COO needs to be able to write messages or pass on verbal instructions that are easily accessible and that no one can misunderstand, of course, but they also have to inspire people. Every word they write or say should help raise the energy throughout the business at all times.

DIPLOMACY

Dropping a COO into an organization can potentially cause huge upheaval, so a COO needs the ability to function as a diplomat from day one, creating harmony in relationships to lay the foundation for when the inevitable healthy conflict occurs. There's a balance in getting all the relevant opinions on the table while also ensuring people like and respect each other. The COO needs to achieve that harmony while also coming into an already-established organization and leading senior people who might have wanted their job or resent no longer reporting to the CEO. The ability to build trust and cultivate personal respect is essential from day one. There will be times when the COO needs to make unpopular decisions for the greater good of the business. If they say what they mean and mean what they say—if they engage in healthy debate and stay focused on the benefit to the team, the vision, the core values, and the health of the company—it will make it easier for others to understand that they aren't arguing or pissing people off for fun, but rather to keep everyone moving forward.

STEADINESS

I've already explained that the stereotype of the crazy visionary CEO is becoming less common; but hell, let's not kid ourselves that it doesn't still exist. A COO shouldn't share that same crazy energy. They should avoid it at all times. They need to keep on an even keel. So what if that makes people think they're a little boring? In reality, they're just more focused.

ENTREPRENEURIALISM

Hello Sign COO Whitney Bouck's advice to her twenty-two-year-old self would be, "Don't try to plan too hard because you may totally miss the best that ever could have happened to you. Be opportunistic."

Whitney encapsulates the entrepreneurial nature of a good COO. They need to be aligned with your vision and focused on how to get there while also being entrepreneurial enough to bob and weave and spot opportunities that fit the vision. Provided they keep in mind their overall direction, a good COO can spot something that wasn't necessarily on the plan, pick it up, and run with it.

If the COO is too rigid with the plan, they'll miss opportunities. On the other hand, entrepreneurs tend to jump from opportunity to opportunity and trust their intuition, which is an approach that won't scale. The COO can't become simply the enforcer of the plan, because forcing people won't help them scale or bolster their cause. The COO needs discipline without sacrificing flexibility or losing sight of their mandate to grow the confidence and skills of the people. Work needs to get done while growing confidence along the way.

COACHING

The COO shouldn't be a go-to referee, just as parents should teach kids to work out their problems rather than mandating solutions. If the COO becomes the referee in a business, they will constantly find themselves involved in conflict, which sets them up for failure. They need instead to focus on coaching, moderating, facilitating discussions, and growing skills so that people can fend for themselves. At the end of the day, the COO can't moderate discussions; they have other work to do.

You catch more flies with honey. It's powerful for leaders to remember when you tell people what to do, you hurt the energy and the organization—but if you can sell them on it, align them with it, and get them excited about it, you'll get the same or better result, with a better energy.

AVAILABILITY

The COO needs to be available to listen to people and help them solve their own problems—though not to serve as a rescuer or dumping ground. Having an open door means both allowing people to come to them and also being able to go out and seek feedback from others in the company.

A COO has much more interaction with the day to day than a CEO. As CEO, particularly as the company scales, you won't have all the tactical answers. You should still connect with people through town halls and skip-level meetings (a strategy I'll discuss in more detail later), but it's the COO's role to be more available to coach and assist with problem-solving.

The COO is a highly visible role within an organization, so you need to hire someone who can command respect within the company with a Level 5 leadership style—as a humble cultural cheerleader and internal champion who will help grow people. They need to have experience but also to check their ego at the door.

When I came into 1-800-GOT-JUNK?, people respected my experience because I'd built other companies before. They asked me what I'd done elsewhere and deferred to my deep domain expertise in franchising, which no one else had. In sharing my experience, I was accessible to a fault. I had more of an open door than necessary. In fact, I had no private office. My desk was out on the floor with everyone else to maintain a connection with everyone in the company. I also spent a lot of time walking around and chatting with people.

CHAPTER 3

WHY HIRE A COO?

"The COO is the CEO's right and left hand. To be most successful, they need to be able to pick up where the CEO leaves off at any given time. A COO is a combination of a mind reader of and a publicist for the CEO."

—LINDSAY SMITH, CHIEF STRATEGY
OFFICER AT TITLE ALLIANCE

The right COO can bring so many benefits to a CEO—the exponential power of the right two in a box, the circle of mutual complementary energy of yin and yang—but only if the CEO knows what they're looking for. Before you know what you need from a COO, you need to understand the kind of CEO you are: who you are, what you do, and what skills you need to bring into the mix.

AN ACTIVITY INVENTORY

CEOs aren't always given to self-reflection—but that's where finding the right second-in-command starts. It might not be an appealing prospect, but think of it this way: hiring a COO is going to make *your* business better, *your* life better, and *you* better. Put the time into pinpointing the changes that will improve your situation most, make your personal situation more sustainable, and make the time you spend on your business more effective. Otherwise, you'll end up hiring someone who would make someone else's life better...but not necessarily *yours*.

The best place to start is with an Activity Inventory, a process I learned from Dan Sullivan at Strategic Coach. Imagine someone followed you around at work for a month and filmed everything you did, from replying to emails and booking flights to chairing meetings and planning budgets. Make a list of all the tasks the camera would capture; then, categorize them in one of four ways:

- I = Incompetent—you suck at it.
- C = Competent—you're okay at it.
- E = Excellent—you have a high level of skill at it, but you don't love it.
- UA = Unique Ability—this is what you're best at and would do for free if you didn't need to feed yourself and your family.

ACTIVITY INVENTORY

Make a List of ALL the Stuff You Do in Your Role During a Typical Quarter, Month, Week & Day

NAME_____ DATE_____

TASKS	C	I	E	U	$/HOUR	S/D/O

KEY

I = Incompetent   U = Unique Ability
C = Competent $/Hr = Hourly Wage
E = Excellent   S, D, or O = Stop, Delegate, or Outsource

The fourth concept is key. Sullivan shows us that Unique Abilities are what allow you to maximize your leverage as a leader by ensuring you only work on projects and areas of the business that you're best suited to. When you're in the realm of your UAs, you love the work and feel energized by it—and the people around you gain energy from you. (If you're spectacular at something but don't get energy from doing it, by the way, don't class it as UA; leave it as an E instead.)

The interesting thing about your UAs is that they're difficult to recognize, because often they're what come most naturally to you. Something might seem so simple you assume that anyone could do it if they just copied what you do—but that's not the case. The whole point is that *not* anyone could do it. Other people might be excellent in your UA area, but that doesn't mean they love doing it. It doesn't mean they would do it for free.

In my case, I'm excellent at sales, but I don't love selling. I find it difficult, and the thought of one more sales call drains me. That's an E for me. My UA is speaking and coaching. If someone could fly me around the world—by private jet so I didn't have to spend all my time in airports—I would do every speaking event I got offered. I'd take my wife with me, and we'd party. I'd fire up audiences, build a brand, and love the process. I don't particularly enjoy the networking and travel (both Es), but speaking is amazing. It's a Unique Ability area for sure.

It wasn't until I worked with Dan that I came to understand my UA—although, looking back, I realize it always involved recruiting and rallying people. I was good at sharing my ideas, starting from winning public speaking contests in second grade. I also loved being on stage and playing the lead role. In 1989, when I was twenty-four, I started helping entrepreneurs through coaching, which I enjoyed—and it was quite a step, given that business and life coaching didn't even become a profession until 1993. In fact, by 1994 I'd already coached 120 entrepreneurs.

Once you've broken all your professional tasks down into the four categories, you can start to identify work you could delegate. The first step is to get all the incompetent and competent tasks off your plate. Stop doing those tasks at once. Outsource them, optimize them, automate them, delegate them to an employee, or hire an Executive Assistant to do them for you.

Now take all the higher-value initiatives you don't love doing, and that are beyond the purview of an EA or regular employee, and put them in a bucket that builds out a job description for a second-in-command. Then you hire a great COO to do the important, high-value work that isn't one of your Unique Abilities.

If that sounds too simple a description, it's really not. Once you know what you need, the whole exercise becomes a lot more straightforward.

FREE UP TIME, MULTIPLY ENERGY, AND GET MORE DONE

The Is, Cs, and even Es on the Activity Inventory don't just reveal the tasks you don't love doing. Those tasks actually sap your energy—and that of the company. If you continue handling them, they'll be a net drain on your organizational capacity.

Just because you've always done something doesn't mean a) it needs to be done, or b) it needs to be done by you. Remember: your to-do list doesn't mean *you* have to do it.

Identify what drains you. I get overwhelmed by running operations, for example, because I've got a million things I want to get started on. I need someone to take all the ideas, prioritize them, run them, and manage the team and resources so we can get more done faster. That shit is key...but it's not my UA.

Once you know what sucks energy from you, you start to crystallize the role you need a second-in-command to fill. The right COO gives you a chance to customize your experience within the business by getting stuff off your desk that has to be done—but, again, not by you. The right COO frees up the time you've been spending on tasks outside your UAs so you can devote more to the areas you love and that give you energy. Then you can feed that energy into the rest of the organization instead of projecting exhaustion, frustration, or stress. That's where a COO adds real leverage.

Part of the CEO's job is to be the chief energizing officer, bringing more positive energy into the business every day. By working only on high-impact areas that give you energy, you will positively affect the whole organization. On the other hand, if you spend time working on roles you hate or aren't good at, your negative energy will be detrimental to everyone.

No one wants to see the CEO slumped over a set of spreadsheets with their head in their hands.

Quantum physics talks about momentum creating momentum, and energy seeking other similar energy. Closer to home, consider how meeting a grumpy barista in the morning can set a negative tone for your day, just as meeting a friendly and positive one can leave you full of energy. If that momentary interaction with a relative stranger can affect your day—which it has been scientifically proven to do—then just think about how important it is for leaders who work with employees for dozens of hours every week to take responsibility for their attitude, impact, and energy.

POSITION FOR GROWTH OR EXIT

Every CEO will eventually exit the company, whether they sell, retire, or die. That's not meant to be mawkish; it's realistic—even though most CEOs feel like they want to lead forever.

A COO can be a key ally in helping to position a company for the CEO's eventual exit. The CEO's obligation to their shareholders is to build an organization that runs itself, doesn't solely rely on the CEO, and can continue on with someone new. That resilience and longevity require having the necessary systems and teams in place. Those systems are best put into place by a COO, to ensure that a company can continue to scale without the current CEO; remember, too, that the COO might be or become the CEO's heir apparent.

A business will always have a CEO, because someone has to be the leader—setting vision and strategy, being accountable, and serving as the legally required signing officer. But it won't always be you.

TRUSTED PARTNER

People assume being a CEO is exciting, but I don't have to tell you that it can also be quite lonely. You're isolated. You can't really tell your Board of Directors or advisors everything that's going on. You can't lean on your employees when you're scared, overwhelmed, overworked, worried, or unsure. You can't even share with your spouse without risking stressing them out if things aren't going well.

The CEO needs to keep their game face on and project excitement and positivity so others feel inspired to follow them—but where can the CEO turn for positivity and reassurance?

The answer is a trusted and reliable COO.

When I spoke with Jim Morrisroe, COO of 15Five, for the *Second in Command* podcast, he recalled his experience as a CEO. It was lonely as hell. As a COO, he sees himself as filling a friendship role for his own CEO, David Hassel. His experience meant that he intuitively recognized the value of filling that void.

No matter how invincible a CEO might feel, they should never underestimate the value of having a partner. You need someone you can trust, be vulnerable with, and open up to. The yin to your yang. You need someone who will tell you the truth, including when they think you're wrong, so you can keep moving forward in a positive direction. It's not simply about your personal feelings; the whole health of the company depends on you feeling—and *being*—happy, stable, and supported. That's how you can provide stability and support to anyone who looks to you for direction—which is everyone.

It's never a good idea to hire people for roles just because you like them. They're not there to get along and hang out; they're there to do a job. For the COO, however, it's *essential* to find someone you like. A CEO needs to make sure they have a COO they'd gladly hang out with, whom they like and respect, and with whom they can share nonwork activities to build their connection, whether playing tennis or golf, going for a run or a bike ride, or cooking barbecue.

That natural affinity helps build mutual trust—and that's how you get to be two in a box.

If it's not there, you risk bringing the wrong energy into the organization.

At 1-800-GOT-JUNK?, Brian and I had an unfair advantage. He'd been the best man at my wedding three months before I started to work with him, so we already knew everything about each other and implicitly trusted each other. Because we'd been in a business group together as entrepreneurs for four years, he'd seen me build two other companies. He knew how I thought and reacted, as well as what my skills were. He knew me so well it was an easy hiring decision once he decided he needed a COO.

You can't always replicate that foundation of friendship, of course. It's rare that you're friendly with exactly the right person you need professionally, but you can build a foundation when you find someone you like and respect. Make sure the person you choose fits what you need temperamentally. Be clear on what you're looking for, including the need for friendship in an often lonely role. The COO should be the CEO's built-in business life preserver, best friend, and sometimes-therapist.

A complete support network for everything in a single individual.

KEEPING UP AND HANDLING DISRUPTION

As we've seen, the role of COO originated with complex businesses like airlines that were highly challenging to run; but recently, COOs have become increasingly common in start-ups and disruptors. Technology, computers, automation, the internet, global organizations, and robotics have given every single business a wake-up call, enabling huge leverage and introducing new business models with exponential growth.

Even highly experienced CEOs can get left behind.

And businesses that don't adapt will die.

As I and others have said many times: if the rate of change outside your business is greater than the rate of change inside your business, then you're out of business.

The COO must not simply understand the rate of change. They must also embrace it—and get out ahead of it.

That's where youth can be an advantage. I was a second-in-command for the first time at age thirty-three. Today, our youngest COO Alliance member, Julia Gordie, is twenty-six. Younger COOs tend to have impressive strength in technology, automation, and digital marketing—even though they often have room to grow on the people side of the business, such as hiring, aligning teams, onboarding, building consensus, and conflict management. That's fine: they can develop these skill sets quickly.

I find it fascinating to watch kids play video games like Minecraft, because the games are all related to the way work gets done in real life: collaborating as a team, talking remotely with people around the world, dividing tasks, project planning, and delivering asynchronously. Young people understand the new ways of working; and if you want your business to succeed, you need to understand, as well.

In the past, people showed up at work at 9:00 a.m. and left at 5:00 p.m., but now many people can work any time over a twenty-four-hour period—and in multiple time zones. They don't have to be at an office; they can work from anywhere around the globe. In fact, I'm currently sitting in Denmark, running the COO Alliance from Europe and proofreading this chapter in a café. When harnessed successfully, these changes massively leverage the power of the COO and, therefore, the CEO.

The CEO is often learning at the same rate as the COO. Entrepreneurial CEOs, in particular, may have an "oh shit" moment when they realize their business is by far the biggest endeavor they've ever undertaken. Maybe the company started as an idea with a friend, but then every day it's a little bigger than the day before...and eventually they realize they need help.

When I became involved with Brian, disruption had just emerged as a business model. We brought a new spin to an old industry. We collected junk with a brand, quality focus areas to connect with the customer, and a premium service. We didn't send garbage collectors to someone's house; we sent clean-cut college students in uniforms and shiny trucks. We did the work for the customer, so they didn't have to lift a finger other than to point at what they wanted hauled away.

Think of all the coffee shops that existed before someone said, "Let's call them Starbucks." There were seventeen thousand independent junk removal services when we started, and we saw the opportunity—with the right systems in place—for branding. We were disruptors, and we harnessed the internet by aiming for 30 percent of our bookings to come from online instead of through the call center. In that way, we changed the industry.

The pace of change continues—just look at the Great Resignation—and businesses have to keep up or die. One of the roles a COO plays is to think strategically and learn from better companies and other industries. That's one of the reasons I started the COO Alliance. Its strength comes from giving COOs access to 170-plus other COOs from seventeen countries who see opportunities differently, leverage technology tools differently, and approach change differently. This cross-pollination inspires, educates, and offers a place to ask questions, so our members can concentrate on working *on* the business and not just *in* it.

A quick note: it's a little ironic, but by starting the COO Alliance, I've become a CEO. It feels very different. Given the choice, at many times I would probably rather still be a COO, as it better suits my natural temperament. But it turns out I approach this new role a bit like I approached my COO role, anyway. I'm a rare breed, combining some entrepreneurial CEO DNA—a bit of mania, a bit of excitement, a bit of marketing pizzazz—with a COO's ability to get things done.

ROCKET FUEL

The right COO is a game changer. As mentioned previously, the power of the right two isn't just a doubling; it's exponential. Brian and I were like nitroglycerin—we ignited productivity and rapid growth.

In October 2000, when Brian shared with me his Vivid Vision—what he then called his Painted Picture—of what his company would look, act, and feel like in 2003, I could see that I knew how to build it. Not only that, but he was okay with moving aside to let me get on with it while he focused on his Unique Abilities. We had remarkable yin and yang in those years, which is why people ran around conferences saying, "I need a Cameron." Everyone around us could see it, too: a strong relationship, real trust, and a great skills match.

We didn't interfere with each other's jobs.

Other times when I've been a second-in-command have been different. At College Pro Painters, I wasn't officially the second-in-command, but rather ran a territory division with full autonomy. Even though I reported to a VP who reported to the CEO, I had so much autonomy that it was like a COO role. When I was president of a private currency company and then the second-in-command for the franchising group of an auto body chain, I again had autonomy—but 1-800-GOT-

JUNK? was the only time I was truly a COO responsible for executing someone else's vision.

Regardless of the exact title for your second-in-command, the right person under the right circumstances can amplify, multiply, and ignite your potential as a leader and the potential of your company.

CHAPTER 4

DO I NEED A COO?

"My goal in my role is to lighten the CEO's load. He shouldn't have to focus on the details, especially as we continue to grow—it's not scalable. I want him to be able to depend on me to ensure that things are being completed to his satisfaction. When that does happen, it feels awesome for both of us."

—REKA VARGA-VIENNE, COO ALLIANCE MEMBER
AND CHIEF OF STAFF AT PHILLIP JEFFRIES LTD.

I like making money—and I like saving money. So, let's start by saving you $250,000 with a simple piece of advice. Don't hire a COO if you don't need one. The right COO in the right situation is transformative—but if they're not necessary, then they represent needless expense, disruption, and commitment.

You'd do better to keep your money.

TRY AN EA FIRST

First up, if all you're really trying to do is to get shit done and free up time, try hiring an EA. It sometimes drives me crazy when people say, "I need a COO." No, what they need is someone who actually has time to *do* stuff—in which case, they should try an EA, who comes a lot cheaper than a COO. They need someone to get a lot of their tasks off their plate.

You may have come across the old business saying that I first heard from my friend Jack Daly: "If you don't have an assistant, you are one."

If you wake up in the morning going, "Ugh," and don't want to face the day, and if you constantly say to yourself, "I just need some help," it's time to look for it. Still, the wrong person can be worse than no one, so plan carefully. Go back to the activity inventory and identify the administrative tasks you can delegate to an EA. See how much that gets off your plate before considering the next level.

If you still have higher-level responsibilities to offload, you may very well need a second-in-command—but you're going to pay them well, so make sure they'll be working on the areas of the business you're either not good at or that drain you of energy.

HIRE THE RIGHT HEADS

You might also not need a COO if what you're really after is a functional head, or heads, to bring expertise to specific domains. If you're having issues with oversight of a particular area or need just one domain off your plate, consider the makeup of your management team before you bring in a second-in-command. A COO can help coordinate the team but is not a substitute for a department head. If you only need help with finance, hire a Head of Finance, who may get the CFO title. If you're lagging on technical stuff, hire a VP of Technology or CTO. Get people who will stick to running their own functional area.

A COO doesn't necessarily have deep expertise in any one domain, but strength in a number of areas. Even if they are particularly good with finance, say—or marketing, or legal—that expertise will likely take a back seat to people and strategy: planning, dealing with other departments, and working with different leadership styles.

Use the activity inventory to identify the tasks, projects, or responsibilities you need to hire for. It may be that they point to a specific function or functions. That's a sign that you don't need a second-in-command yet, just a very strong VP of IT, finance, marketing, or sales. It's much cheaper and easier to find such a person (plus, it's also easier to exit them from the organization when they've done their job).

The time to hire a COO is when your activity inventory leaves you with multiple overflowing buckets of tasks. That's when you need strong, coordinating leadership to help orchestrate them all.

Hiring a COO is a much greater commitment than hiring a functional head, and you need to get it right.

CUT BACK YOUR CORE

If you're thinking about hiring a COO because you can't keep visibility across all your projects, you could always flip the problem. Perhaps rather than hiring a COO to handle the projects you can't, you should consider whether you have too many core projects. You might be better off scaling back. Take some time to figure out whether your core projects are truly core.

Remember, of course, that if you do hire a COO, they might come in and quickly identify that you have too many projects in the mix. If that happens, they'll offer suggestions to streamline, with an eye toward working on the critical few projects versus the important many.

GO FRACTIONAL

Another possibility to consider before hiring a full-time COO is hiring a Fractional COO. This is a comparatively recent development that has rapidly established its own core niche because it's so useful to many businesses. A Fractional COO is usually a former senior exec who has chosen to work for multiple companies rather than just one. A company usually hires them to coach an executive team, to lead a core project—or to do whatever is required—but doesn't need them on a day-to-day basis. Many COOs get started this way before they become permanent somewhere—if they ever do.

A Fractional COO can be really useful for small or midsize companies that don't need or can't afford a full-time COO. It allows them to scale up without paying a full-time salary. It frees up their teams to execute while making sure there is a clear path ahead, with the right systems and operations to bring growth. The companies can leverage all the benefits of a full-time COO in the specific areas needed and continue to look after the rest of the business themselves.

Working with a Fractional COO also gives a CEO a chance to analyze how they might eventually work with a full-time COO when the time is right—and it gives them a taste of the contribution the right COO could make to their business. In fact, when I started coaching CEOs back in 2007, I called my company BackPocket COO—the idea being that I was in their back pocket, and they could pull me out for advice and coaching when they needed me. The concept worked, as I had three companies in my first year paying me $120,000 each to be their Fractional COO. It's something I no longer do—but I loved it at the time.

A HIRE MUST ADD VALUE

You've hired an EA, you've got strong leaders for all your functions, you've made sure your core projects are all adding value, you've tried working with a Fractional COO—and your activity inventory is still telling you that you need to hire a second-in-command.

The next step is to hire a COO, right? Not necessarily. Hiring a COO is such a huge step that it's worth pausing to ask yourself the last key question: can I afford to make this hire?

The answer works on different levels, including the bottom line: will this hire pay for itself? There's no point in hiring a COO unless they will add more value than the cost of their salary. As a rule of thumb, you should be looking for every employee to return a minimum of 2X—and preferably 4X—on their pay because you'll need that increase in gross margin the company makes to pay for them and break even.

A COO is no different—though their value goes beyond a dollar amount, which makes it essential for you to be clear on your objective.

There are four main reasons to bring in a COO:

- to increase efficiency
- to make employees or customers happier
- to grow the economic value of the company
- to grow profitability

Any advance a COO makes in those areas adds to the COO's value. Do you want to increase sale value as you build toward an exit, for instance, or are you aiming to free up your own time? If it's the latter, the COO might not directly drive more profitability but could take fifty hours a week off your plate so you could spend ten more elsewhere. If you can afford it, it can be worthwhile to forgo some profit to gain a significant amount of time.

A COO IS FOR THE LONG TERM

As we'll see later, bringing in a COO can add a potential cost in terms of organizational upheaval. Ask yourself whether that's a price worth paying to make the hire. You're dropping a giant boulder into the pond of your organization. It's bound to create ripples. Hiring a second-in-command is not like onboarding a management team role that slips in almost unnoticed. If you already have strong departmental heads with good domain expertise, then the COO's arrival can easily put people's noses out of joint. Be prepared for resentment, pushback, and even resignations.

The third potential cost you need to be able to afford is commitment. Hiring a COO is a decision with a long-term impact; if you're just looking for a way out of a short-term crisis, a consultant will likely be a better fix, as well as easier to hire and let go—and won't come with any of the close personal relationship dynamics that will come with a COO.

PART 2

HIRING
A COO

CHAPTER 5

STARTING THE PROCESS

"It's all about the people. Everything that you will do and no matter what level of success you're trying to achieve, it will depend on the people you have supporting you. [Figure out] the types of people you want, and try your best to get the hiring right."

—ROMAN COWAN, COO ALLIANCE MEMBER AND
COO OF COLLEGE HUNKS HAULING JUNK

You've checked your management team, your structure, whether you have too many core projects, and whether there are holes to fill. You may have tried consultants, new function roles, or an EA. If you still need a second-in-command, then it's time to hire the perfect COO for you and the business.

There are a number of ways to do that, including word of mouth, posting a job listing, or contacting a recruiter. Before you can start on any of them, however, you need to sit down and figure out exactly the type of person who will fill the need you have identified—and then how to find that person.

Your activity inventory has helped identify your Unique Abilities (UAs) and where you are lacking. Now continue a similar exercise to determine the type of person who would be the yin to your yang. Simply put, their Unique Abilities and weaknesses are likely the opposite of yours—and they share your core values for the organization. Consider the domains they'd oversee and the personality traits that would complement yours.

The CEO and COO tend to have strengths in different areas. That creates a well-rounded package, but unless the fit is perfect, those differences can also lead to tension. That's why I go back to repeating that a CEO has to truly know themselves to hire the right partner. The deeper your understanding of your skills, weaknesses, and Unique Abilities—as well as the areas you want to delegate—the better your chances of finding the person who likes doing what you don't and is great in the areas where you suck.

Defining such a person might sound daunting, but it doesn't have to be a long, drawn-out process. Your activity inventory, UAs, and core needs provide the parameters. A couple of focused hours spent using them as a framework should give you a good idea of what you're looking for. That's the information you'll use to write a job description that is extremely specific, including the behavioral traits you require in a second-in-command—which will depend on the areas of the business reporting to this person, as well as the core responsibilities and metrics for which they'll be accountable. Specify what you want them to oversee; equally, make it clear what you'll be keeping under your purview and don't want them to touch.

This is where understanding yourself is key to preventing you from falling into stereotypes, assumptions, and lazy thinking.

There's a popular belief that CEOs should be gregarious cult-like figures—Steve Jobs is one of the best-known examples—but you don't have to be like that. Nearly any type of personality can make a successful CEO, and it's fine. You don't have to play a role. If culture is where you lag, then accept that fact and delegate culture to a COO. It's not a sign of weakness. It doesn't matter who does it—just as long as it gets done.

If you're a strong engineer who invented the product, and what you really want is to stay involved on the technical side, then your UA might not be cheerleading. In that case, specify that you need someone who can be an outward-facing culture person while leaving the technical aspects of the product well alone.

There's almost no part of the business you can't assign to a COO: legal, finance, engineering, culture. The division of labor is entirely driven by UAs and personality—although the CEO obviously still needs to attend board meetings and planning meetings that require top-level input.

In theory, too, a CEO can also keep as much for themselves as they want, as long as they have the bandwidth and enjoy doing the work.

After all, it's *their* business. That's especially true for entrepreneurs.

They just need to make sure they're thinking strategically about the best use of their time and energy.

TWO IN A BOX AT THE BOTTOM, NOT THE TOP

It's easy to approach hiring a second-in-command as hiring a leader. That's not how I see it. A COO is a supporter as much as a leader—which is exactly how I see the role of the CEO, too. When you've got your two in a box—a yin-yang combination of CEO and COO—that box belongs at the bottom of any org chart, not the top. The CEO and COO have a joint mission to support the people on the front lines and their customers. They're the two most senior people in the business, but that doesn't mean they should be at the top telling everyone what to do. Instead, they should be serving the organization by removing obstacles, providing support, and aligning and inspiring people. I visualize org charts upside down, with the CEO and COO at the bottom, supporting the other C-level and VP roles above them who are supporting and growing the managers above them, and so on.

It's true that our grandfathers wouldn't recognize that definition of a CEO or COO. But it's also true that their old-school hierarchical business model doesn't work anymore. Most people know that intuitively.

LEANING INTO THE FUTURE

To help get clarity about the ideal person you're looking for, try "leaning out into the future." Imagine your business three years from now. What's your Vivid Vision of what the company will look, act, and feel like? How will the org chart change to get you there?

That clarity allows you to answer the question, *"What do I need in a second-in-command?"*

As the Cheshire Cat says in *Alice in Wonderland*, "If you don't know where you're going, any road will take you there." Leaning out into the future helps you find the right road. It allows you to figure out where you're going so you can reverse-engineer that future...and figure out the people who will help make it come true. Maybe the future holds growth through acquisitions or a move into multiple new markets. Strategizing those steps will highlight gaps both in the structure and systems of the business and in your personal skill set.

When Brian leaned out into the future thinking of building 1-800-GOT-JUNK?, we realized he needed to launch franchise sales and coaching programs; build a marketing calendar, budget, and campaigns; create a leadership training program for his people; and do recruiting and interviewing. He also realized he didn't know how to make those initiatives happen—and that it would be much more effective to find someone who had the skills he needed rather than trying to learn them himself.

That's why he brought me in.

Your plan for the future doesn't have to be perfect, so don't get stuck on details. You simply need a clear direction for the company and an understanding of what it will look like, so you can envision where a new second-in-command would sit. And you don't have to shape the future alone.

Sit down with your leadership team, ask questions, and come up with a working plan.

YOU DON'T HAVE TO KNOW EVERYTHING

Whenever I used to ask my mom how to spell a word, her response was "D-I-C-T-I-O-N-A-R-Y." She was smart.

Traditional schooling does us all a disservice by teaching us that we should aspire to be the person who has all the answers. It's a ridiculous goal. As Mom understood, you don't need to know stuff. You just need to know where you can find answers. Kids increasingly realize they don't have to know all the answers but only how to find the answers quickly. That's why so many of them are turning their backs on college: they realize there's no need to spend huge amounts of time and money learning information they can find out easily for free.

It's the same in business. More than ever, effective business leaders recognize what my friends Dan Sullivan and Ben Hardy outlined in their book *Who Not How*: you solve problems by finding the right people, not by endlessly having to learn how to do everything.

Dan and Ben explain that business leaders no longer have to know how to tackle every situation. Rather, they have to know how to find other people to do it for them. It's a powerful and common-sense approach; but it also requires overcoming many of the ideas we were brought up with.

It's not as if I see a lot of teachers running large companies.

The school system teaches us that if we're bad at something, we should get a tutor, work at it, and get good at it. The reality is that, if you're really bad at something and you work at it, you'll still likely only ever become average.

If you're really bad at something, you don't have to work at it. Instead, you can get a COO who's great at it. At a stroke, you've leveraged your combined abilities to address the company's needs in a different way.

It should be a relief for a CEO to realize they don't have to invest in getting better at skills. They can just find the right person instead of continuing to struggle, even if the tasks are those that fall under the "traditional" auspices of the CEO.

No CEO should feel they need to master areas of their business that don't play to their Unique Abilities.

Your exact list of what you need a COO to do will be highly unique—but you'd be a fool if it didn't start with all the things you suck at or hate. That's the whole point of the exercise.

If you're great at strategy, the COO had better be great at execution. If you're a natural at execution, then the COO needs to do a great deal of strategic thinking to balance that out. Just because you're the CEO doesn't mean you have to be great at stuff other CEOs are great at. You might absolutely suck at strategy, which means you can hire a second-in-command who can fill that gap.

Strategy is a skill and a way of thinking and asking questions. It involves connecting, networking, and masterminding, and not all CEOs are good at those elements or enjoy doing them. Some CEOs are amazing engineers focused on technology who have weaknesses in strategy, vision, culture, and people. No problem. Just hire a COO who excels in those areas.

Just because you're the boss doesn't mean you need to do

everything the business needs. It's far better to find the right person to follow through. Traditionally, CEOs have been the visionaries, but you can turn that dynamic on its head if doing so will play to your strengths. Traditionally, men worked outside the home and women stayed home with kids, but now many families find it's better to have a stay-at-home dad and a breadwinner mom.

There are no rules.

CORE VALUES AND BEHAVIORAL TRAITS

The CEO sets the core values for the company and needs a COO who supports them. They might be the result of conscious decisions and even consultation throughout the business, or they might be embodied by the CEO's own personal conduct. To hire the right second-in-command, however, a CEO needs to figure out what the core values *are* and how to identify them in a potential hire.

It's far easier to recruit someone who already lives by the same core values than it is to take someone on who doesn't and then persuade them to fall in line.

The key is to figure out what are core values, and what are values that are simply nice to have. The difference is that core values are make or break. Not only do you live by them under all circumstances, but you are willing to fire people who break them. That's the key. Other cultural qualities might be a bonus or an aspiration, but they're not core values.

That's a distinction most CEOs will agree with.

I use the example of growing up in the Roman Catholic church. When my dad told me people confessed to the priest all the bad things they'd done, I assumed the priest spanked them. When dad explained that they just had to say some prayers to make everything okay, I concluded that they clearly weren't breaking the church's core values.

In my family, if we broke the core values, we got a spanking.

As well as spelling out the values you need in a second-in-command, you should specify the necessary behavioral traits they will need to mesh with yours and the company as a whole. If you're focused and shy, are you looking for a gregarious leader? Do you need someone more detail-oriented, or someone focused on the bigger picture? As we'll see later, these needs sometimes change over time—which is why I'm no longer COO at 1-800-GOT-JUNK?.

LIKE A MARRIAGE

The closest equivalent in ordinary life to finding a COO in business is finding a spouse. Once you're crystal clear on what you're looking for and can describe it, you will pass over anyone who doesn't fit the bill, because a bad marriage is not worth it.

When you draw up your job description of the right COO, you're not creating a list of "nice to haves." You're listing the essentials that are 100 percent required. A candidate without all of them need not bother to apply. You're looking for trust, core values, behavioral traits, skillset, strengths, and desires that complement yours, all in a package that comes with a personal chemistry that might grow into a deep friendship.

Bear in mind another parallel with a marriage. When you finally end up with the right person, you're not going to be able to change their personality. Focus on exactly what makes the right match to get the perfect fit right off.

If this process sounds high-stakes, it is. It can feel like a hellish ordeal to go through. Remember, though, that you don't have to go through it alone. You have a whole leadership team to help you. You don't even have to be the person who conducts the interviews. You can use an executive search firm, your board of advisors, or members of your leadership team—as long as you're all clear on who you're looking for.

NOT JUST "A CAMERON"

I'm constantly asked to be a COO for companies, and I just laugh. For one thing, most people who ask can't afford me—yet they really need to find a way to hire a truly competent COO. For another 90 percent of the CEOs who ask me to be their COO, I'd be a horrible fit.

I can see that because I understand myself and where I add value. To successfully hire a second-in-command, a CEO needs to be able to see that, too.

People who simply assume they can plug me—or someone like me—into their business to solve their problems don't understand the nature of a strong working partnership. Sometimes, I don't have the skills to work in their business or don't like doing the tasks they need done. Sometimes, I don't have the required behavioral traits. Sometimes, there's no trust factor.

I can see those mismatches where my yin doesn't fit someone else's yang, but the CEOs who approach me can't. That's because they aren't thinking about the situation in the right way. They're simply trying to plug an execution hole with anyone, and they've heard my name. They've not considered what shape that hole is and who can best fill it.

CHAPTER 6

HOW TO HIRE

"From when we first started talking seriously about the opportunity to when I joined was about four months. By the time I joined, I felt like we already knew each other very well."

—SCOTT SHRUM, COO ALLIANCE MEMBER AND
PRESIDENT AND COO AT HENNESSEY DIGITAL

Because COOs are not often transferable from one organization to another, finding them isn't always easy. There's no central casting where you can hire the perfect fit, so it's usually a tough recruitment search. In addition, the top-level people you need are rarely unemployed—only 5 percent of them are ever out of work—and they're likely not looking for a new post. That means you'll have to poach them.

The right search firm can help with that, in addition to the usual online job postings and engaging your external network to help the hunt.

INTERNAL VS. EXTERNAL HIRES

The first decision to make is whether you want to promote from within or hire from outside. An internal hire can make sense when a company requires deep technical knowledge or industry focus. Moving from one company to another within an industry can also work, although it's harder to transfer COO skills across industries. So, if your organization inhabits a specific niche and you have strong talent, then promoting from within can be a good choice.

However, internal hires can go wrong when employees feel there's nepotism at work or that the CEO is playing favorites. Hurt feelings can inhibit productivity. An internal COO needs the preparation and skill set to manage their former peers.

Hiring internally also means, obviously, that you're limiting the pool of candidates and might miss out on better fits you would have found outside. Going with the easy hire feels better than doing the work—it's the "devil you know"—but settling for a mediocre COO is a mistake. If you hire from within, make sure you fully know the person so there are no doubts about whether they can live up to the role.

Don't just think, "We'll give them a try."

You would never hire an external candidate and let them "try." That's just another way of saying you're going to give them a chance to potentially wreak havoc on your teams.

There's data that shows that the cost of hiring the wrong person is 15X their annual salary. So if you're paying them $250,000 a year, it's going to cost you $3 to $4 million per year to have them there in terms of other employees not joining you, opportunity costs, time lag, misinformation, bad decisions being made by the wrong person, a board that won't invest because they don't trust that person, and relationship issues between you and them that everyone else in the company is seeing.

It's kind of like mom and dad fighting. The kids just don't want to be around them.

If you can hire well from within your company, good for you! If you can't, bear in mind what I've said before—that the best outside candidates already have jobs and will need to be poached. Both approaches can have their pros and cons.

Whether a COO needs to come from within a specific industry depends on both the industry and what the business needs. Many companies don't require strong technical skills, so a COO doesn't necessarily need expertise in the exact business space. In my case, I knew nothing about junk removal but lots about customer engagement and franchising. I excelled at promoting franchise partner success, and people bought franchises because they could see my passion. That probably means I could franchise any business in the home services space—but it doesn't mean I have the skills to build, say, a technology company.

I also fit the brand and the CEO. In the past, you used to hear the adage, "Hire for attitude; train for skill." That approach won't work anymore. Now you have to hire for both cultural fit and skill.

If you hire for just one or the other, they'll both fail.

COO Alliance member Scott Shrum says of his transition to COO at Hennessey Digital, "My previous job was as president of a small, privately held company that was at about the same size and life stage that Hennessey Digital was when I joined. Even though that company was in a different industry, my experience of leading it through a decade of growth made me a good fit for the role."

Someone with a background in apparel who doesn't know the car industry can't be the COO of a car company—there's just too much subject-matter expertise missing. However, it's easy for the COO of a restaurant chain to go to another restaurant chain, regardless of the type of cuisine. In the same way, someone who has built a technology company could probably build another one.

PREPARE FOR CHALLENGES

Bringing in an external hire to oversee existing employees is like an advanced chess move. You need to be thinking three or four moves ahead. You need to notify employees of the process before it starts and persuade them to feel excited to work for this new leader. You may need to show some of them that they would not have been the right person for the role. You should also be transparent about compensation, because it's a big issue—and because everyone will soon find out what the COO earns anyway.

Plan and have all those discussions before the issues come up.

Bringing in an outsider as second-in-command creates an inherent challenge. The newcomer hasn't witnessed the history of the company, how its DNA was formed, how its idiosyncrasies developed, or how the different leadership styles work together. There are thousands of elements insiders take for granted that no outsider can hope to understand in the beginning. However, coming in with the right core values and strong technical skills can set them up for success—if they have the aptitude to learn the cultural side of the business.

It only works to bring in someone from the outside if they have strength and depth in industry IP. On the other hand, a COO who grows up inside of the business and understands the culture and history deeply might lack the same technical depth of experience as someone who has been working elsewhere.

A COO BY ANY OTHER NAME

It might seem a minor consideration, but a CEO looking for second-in-command should consider what to call them in any job posting. I actually prefer the term "second-in-command" over COO, partly because it gives definition, clarity, and flexibility in hiring—and partly because the options can be misleading.

A Chief Operating Officer, for example, might not have anything to do with operations. In the same way, although you can be the CEO of a company whether you lead one person or five thousand people, you likely wouldn't call a second-in-command a COO in a twenty- or thirty-person company. A better title for that second-in-command might be Director or VP of Operations.

Companies' searches can get sloppy or expensive if they start giving out titles too early.

The job title has to match both the responsibilities of the role and the compensation you're willing to pay, which are both linked to the size of your business. In a fifty-person company, say, you might be hiring a Director of Operations, a General Manager, an Operations Manager, or a VP of Operations.

The bigger the title you give away, the more responsibilities the person should have—because they'll expect their compensation to be based on their title. For instance, at the time of this writing, Salary.com says the average COO salary is $464,000; while the average Director of Operations makes $180,000. I take those figures with a pinch of salt because I feel recruiting sites inflate them to raise people's expectations and get attention. Realistically, I'd expect to have to pay about $300,000 for a COO and $130,000 for a Director of Operations; for a VP Operations it might be more like $180,000.

To see what COOs typically get paid, visit: https://cooalliance. com/salary-survey. In return for filling out a short salary survey, you'll receive a comprehensive data set for second-in-command roles around the world.

A COO, a Director of Operations, or a VP of Operations could all be the Head of Operations, so ensure the title you give the role aligns with what you're looking for. People will base their salary expectations on the title, not necessarily on the details of their roles and responsibilities.

Smaller companies can get lazy about giving out titles and letting people call themselves what they want—but again, they should be aware that different titles come with different salaries attached. Be very clear with any executive search firm regarding whether you're hiring a true COO, a VP of Operations, a Director of Operations, or someone else. Recruiters will look at different talent pools depending on the answer.

SCORECARD AND JOB DESCRIPTION

The first requirement for your job search is a scorecard for your COO. Once you know what you're looking for, create a scorecard for the role. There's a sample one in the appendix that you can use as a launch point—but remember that there's no such thing as a template scorecard, because there's no such thing as a template COO.

Sometimes CEOs ask me, "Can you send me a COO scorecard so I can copy it and start recruiting?" No! That's like them saying, "Can you send me your description of your perfect partner so I know who to go out and start dating?"

My idea of a perfect partner is likely very different from yours. A CEO can have as much help as they need in the search process; but, as the leader, it comes down to them to define who they're looking for.

Don't get married to someone else's idea of a perfect spouse.

Base the scorecard on asking yourself: what are the top five things the COO would have to get done in their first year for the hire to be a success? You can rate your prospects using the COO Alliance's eight core areas: vision, strategic plan, people systems, meetings, financial systems, job-related skills, mentors, and company culture.

The scorecard lays out whether a hire will fit with the organization—and how you'll measure success.

This part of the process requires your thoughtful vision and full engagement; don't phone it in. Use the steps from the previous chapter to make sure you know your own needs and temperament as well as the Unique Abilities and temperament that would complement yours. Otherwise, you're unlikely to find a good candidate. Technology means you have a wider reach in your search than ever before—but preparation, self-knowledge, and leaning into the future can't be automated.

The goal is to recruit, interview, and hire someone who doesn't just *know how* to do the work on the scorecard but has *actually done it* before. To use a left-field analogy, pretend you were hiring a swimmer. (Why? Who knows?) Do you want someone who knows all four strokes, how to win an Olympic gold medal, and how to break a world record—or do you want someone who has *won* a gold medal, even in just one stroke? You go for the experience. In theory, most people know how to win a gold medal in swimming—but suck at doing it.

You'll need to dig deeply enough to make sure a candidate has truly done the work—not that they just know about it from school or books.

Once you've established your scorecard, you need to write your job description. It has to be written in such a way that when your perfect COO reads it, they think, "Fuck yeah, I am all in." If you swear in real life, swear in your job description. Say, "I'm a CEO who's slightly manic and who fucking swears a little bit too much." That way, if somebody comes in and goes,

"I don't like that you swore," it's "Cool, see ya. I don't love that I swear, either; but if you're going to work with me, we have to at least gel for a starting point."

Write your first draft of your job description like you're telling your best friend about the role. Then, hand it to a marketing person or a copywriter—a really good one. Pay a thousand bucks to have a copywriter make that job description pop off the page like the best sales copy you've ever written in your life. We would never write our own website copy or landing pages without using a copywriter, so why would we use a job description that HR wrote? HR? They suck at marketing. They're process people. They're about policies and procedures. You need a copywriter to write your job description so that the right people will look at it and go, "Hell yeah, I want that role"—and the wrong people will look at it and think, "Not if it was the last job on Earth."

Now it's a question of getting the job description in front of as many people as possible. Share a link to it with your entire network, including on LinkedIn and Facebook, and ask your employees to do the same. Contact any business or mastermind groups you belong to and send it to them. Share it with your entire email list.

If you've clearly described the role, people will immediately have a sense of who would be the perfect fit and start directing likely people toward you.

DIFFERENCES BY BUSINESS SIZE

Your search for a second-in-command depends somewhat on the size of your business.

- **Small (under 50 employees).** The CEO is often looking for someone who can simply get work done, because they are too busy or need someone who knows how to scale. The COO generally comes in to build the first management team, followed by the first leadership team. Those COO roles tend to be for a jack of all trades, someone who can handle a wide variety of work, project manage, and stay on top of all the moving parts as the company scales. At this size, the COO is telling everyone what to do.

- **Medium (50 to 200 employees).** These firms generally need someone who can build a strong leadership team, recognize the different needs between a leadership team and a management team, and bring domain expertise. They can think strategically, but this role may be the biggest thing they've ever done. They must be good at developing people and growing the skills of the team, and they probably need strong financial acumen the bigger the business gets.

- **Large (200 to 500 employees).** These businesses need an increasingly seasoned COO, and the role no longer involves telling people what to do. Instead, the COO is collaborating, problem-solving, removing obstacles, and thinking in an increasingly strategic way.

- **Enterprise Level (500 and up).** This is beyond my sweet spot. All bets are off. But thanks for reading. ;) And once you hire them, your COO can still join the COO Alliance.

SEARCH FIRMS

Given that external hires usually mean poaching, an executive search firm can help you identify and approach A-list candidates. Most A-players are never out looking for a job. They're not scouring LinkedIn or industry job boards. They don't have a résumé to hand to you. Unless someone puts your posting in front of them, they won't see it. Qualified search firms know where those good people are and can reach out to see if they're interested.

Expect a recruiter to set up a conversation—but not to send along a résumé. I haven't had a résumé since 1989 because I haven't needed one. Many A-players don't have résumés, either, because *they* don't need them. Don't focus on what's on paper; focus on what candidates say and how they say it. Just talk to them about what they've been doing, their experience, how their current company poached them, and why they left the company they were with before that. Understand their motivators and incentives—not just so you can bring them on board but also so that you can prevent them from leaving in the future.

To reach the right people, the executive recruiter needs the scorecard and job description for the role. The scorecard should give full clarity on what the person will be responsible for and how their success will be measured. The job posting should be at least 90 percent perfect. If you haven't had it copyedited, the recruiter might have a copyeditor polish it, but they can't fill big gaps around compensation, possible titles, or reporting structure.

Because of the diversity of COOs, there aren't any one-stop-shop COO recruitment firms. However, there are qualified firms that recruit for COOs in addition to other C-level roles.

I refer senior searches to four great executive search firms all the time. They are not names you'll know already, so if you'd like an introduction, email me (info@cameronherold. com). The first firm I work with specializes in the $200,000–$350,000 range and is amazing at finding good, solid, seasoned COOs or VPs of Operations. I've referred thirty clients to them over the past ten years. They have an intense attention to culture and are careful not to disclose information to candidates they don't think are the right cultural fit.

I also have a firm that only recruits Virtual Assistants and Executive Assistants, if you're not yet ready for a second-in-command and want to buy some time and free up some of yours.

I categorize the rest according to compensation level: one only recruits for $500,000-plus roles for very seasoned executives, and another works in the $120,000–$180,000 range for more junior people. Again, simply email me for an intro—I'm happy to help you out.

When you're doing job postings, be sure to include the compensation in the job posting itself, because it'll help attract the right people and make the recruiter's job easier. The right firm can do a great job referring qualified candidates—but only in their own range. If they only recruit from the most senior people and you want someone midlevel, you're fishing in the wrong pond and you won't get the right catch.

You need to do the work on the front end to establish where

you need to get to. Remember the wisdom of the Cheshire Cat: if you don't know where you're going, any road will take you there.

If you don't know what you're looking for, any executive search firm will do—until you realize you've just agreed to pay $420,000 for what should have been a $200,000 job.

If you use an executive search firm, don't just jump on the candidates they send right away. Some firms are more interested in getting you to choose one of their candidates—it's how they get paid—than in finding the absolute best person available. This is why I love the firms I introduce my clients to. They know they're sending us great prospects, but they also know we're really going to interview them hard, too.

Stress-test them. Tell them, "Thank you for sending all those amazing candidates, but I still want to do our process." They might insist that they've already run their own process, and the candidates they've sent you are plug-and-play. Making a decision based on their assessment alone is like picking someone to marry from three possible blind dates lined up by a stranger.

Complete your own process, as well. You're interviewing your work spouse, so do your own reference checks, screen the resumes, and check for culture fit. A search firm will send you good, solid, qualified leads—but you can't just accept them without doing your own legwork.

To have the highest chance of success, make sure you fully educate the search firm on the Vivid Vision for the company, what you're building, and the scorecard for the role. Spend the time on the front end to ensure they fully understand the leads they're generating and will only send you their best-fit candidates. If they're crystal clear on the role, the company, the culture fit, and who you are as a CEO, they'll do a much better job.

You're not their only client, so it's important to train them on exactly what you need and which candidates would make a good fit. That requires far more than simply handing them a job description and telling them to go find your princess or prince. Have multiple members of your team brief them so they get the whole picture.

NETWORKING

In the past, becoming a CEO was about capabilities and connections. You might remember how every city or town had business clubs, mostly for men in jackets and ties, as a way for the power elite to pay for access to the closed community. They were members of golf clubs and tennis clubs for the same reason. Education might have been democratized, but networking remained the preserve of the elite. A CEO who needed to recruit a COO had a small pool to fish in.

Today, the pool is much larger and technology—the Internet and social media—makes it easy to cast a wide net. CEOs still tend to be smart and capable, but the role is more democratic, and they can leverage the strengths of a far greater group of candidates, including men (and women) who would never have been allowed in the old business clubs.

Twenty years ago, recruiting required a newspaper ad,

search firms, employee referrals, asking around at the club, and keeping your fingers crossed that someone lived nearby. Today, you can post a job on Facebook or LinkedIn and find great candidates who will compensate for your weaknesses, even though they live in another city, another state—or even another country—especially when you have really strong job postings written to magnetize the talent you want to hire.

In the past, work almost exclusively happened in person, so candidates for posts had to be within commuting distance or be willing to move. Now they can come from virtually anywhere, depending on the scope of the job. I spoke with the COO of a 310-person company on our *Second in Command* podcast about this. Despite being the second-in-command, she is the only employee who lives in Seattle; her team is spread over six countries, and the majority live in New York City. As long as talent can be integrated, fits culturally, can get the job done, and is willing to work for what you're willing to pay, it doesn't matter where they live.

That expands your choices exponentially.

When Brian needed a COO for 1-800-GOT-JUNK?, he had to rely on his own network. The entire face of the business would have been different if he didn't happen to know me. I know the other candidate he considered, and I know that without me the company never would have reached even $10 million. I recruited someone who became the first franchisee and remains the biggest franchisee to this day, doing gross revenue already exceeding $25 million.

Brian didn't know me entirely by chance. He knew me because

he was okay with learning from others and not always being the most knowledgeable person in the room; he had set out deliberately to cultivate his network of other CEOs. We met through the Entrepreneurs' Organization (EO), and today there are far more of these mastermind communities. I would strongly recommend that every CEO should get involved with at least one thought-leadership community such as EO, Young Presidents' Organization (YPO), Vistage, Genius Network, Baby Bathwater, War Room, Mastermind Talks, or Strategic Coach. I've been a member of all of them, some for seven years.

It's a CEO's responsibility to cultivate their network for the benefit of the company.

CEO networks are much stronger in the United States and Canada than anywhere else in the world. In other countries, there's almost no entrepreneurial support system (Italy's one example). There is some global reach with YPO and EO, but whereas there might be fifty different communities for entrepreneurs in North America, the UK might only have a handful. In any case, CEOs should join one, and the COO Alliance was created so seconds-in-command can grow their network, skills, and confidence, as well.

Networking and the democratization of knowledge are powerful tools—but only if you use them. A shovel doesn't dig a hole on its own; it just sits in the corner unless someone picks it up and uses it. Leverage the tools—collaboration, democratization, access to information, outsourcing—because the alternative is to fall into the same trap as the many CEOs who still defer to the smartest person in the room or hire the MBA who "knows it all."

They need to take their heads out of their asses, grab the shovel, and start digging.

VIRTUAL BENCH

I once had dinner with a talented executive and told him, "I know I'll hire you one day, but it's not now." I told him I'd keep his résumé on file. Six months later, when I was recruiting, I reached out to him. Christopher Bennett was surprised I'd kept my word, but I hired him, and he worked for us for years; he's a close personal friend to this day. And he was an iconic part of our growth.

Even when I'm not actively recruiting, I constantly keep my eye open for people who could work well at my company and whom I'd like to contact in the future. I call it my "virtual bench."

I keep my eyes and ears open regarding potential positions that might open up in an organization, as well as potential fits for those future roles. I'm keenly aware that the best people probably already have jobs, of course, but I'm okay with taking them away from an average company and bringing them to a great one. In my mind, it's no different from taking a great soccer player and moving them to a better team. The best teams are always trying to recruit players—and the best players are always trying to play for the best teams.

Recruiting employees from other companies is like sport. I do it on weekends for fun. And it's a full-contact activity.

Your COO is working somewhere today. They work for one

of the top companies to work for, one of the best managed and fastest growing companies. They work for a client like yours, and you go and poach those people. You have to look to recruit and bring those people into your organization—not just as COOs, but across your organization. Some of you already know your COO candidates; you likely met them years ago.

THE INTERVIEW PROCESS

Hiring a capable COO will test the interviewing, recruiting, and hiring competency of any organization. I devote a whole core module of my Invest in Your Leaders course to interviewing and doing the reference checks because those steps are so crucial to finding and vetting the best candidate.

Don't rely on HR. That might sound counterintuitive, but HR are not the best folks to interview and recruit a COO. Their role is to support the search by getting the job posting in front of as many eyes as possible, soliciting video submissions, and setting up the first round of group interviews. But the actual interviews should be conducted by the board, the leadership team, and the CEO. They're the only people who can hire a COO. HR doesn't have that level of capacity to do senior-hire interviewing.

The actual interviews can be held over Zoom or in-person, but they must be rigorous, and the process should involve more people than just the CEO—and should possibly include outside advisors (I've been called in numerous times to interview COOs on behalf of different CEOs).

Any of the new COO's potential direct reports should participate in the interviews, because they'll be best placed to figure out the culture fit and any energy issues of their new leader. If they interview candidates in a panel format of around three people, they can have a more lively, less threatening discussion than in a one-on-one interview and gain more insight. The candidate will also get a better sense of the kinds of teams they'd be leading.

VIDEO SUBMISSIONS

The interview process starts with HR gathering as many résumés as possible from great people. Send the candidates the Vivid Vision for your company, along with a recent article about the company in the media, and ask them to send a three- to four-minute video about why and how they think they can help make the Vivid Vision come true.

I don't even read the résumés until I receive that video submission, which I use as the initial screening. It doesn't matter what skills they have unless they feel like the right culture fit. If they're not excited about the Vivid Vision of where the company is going, any interview will be a waste of time.

A total of ten videos is an ideal starting point. (Ten *résumés* aren't enough, however, because half of them will be from people who are playing the odds and sending their résumés out everywhere; they don't know enough about your company and haven't visualized themselves in the role, so they're another time waste.) If you're using recruiters, tell them to share the Vivid Vision and get the video submissions before you start considering the candidates. If a candidate won't take the time to submit a video, don't take the time to interview them.

By screening the videos for culture fit before reviewing résumés, you'll interview fewer people and in a more thorough way, because you already know they're solid. You end up with a high-quality short list with whom you can do a deep dive on actual skills and experience.

In the initial interview, probe each candidate's culture fit first to make sure they already live the organization's core values, have the behavioral traits you're looking for, and truly only want to work in the areas of the business that the CEO does not.

That last is crucial. You don't want to hire someone with a burning desire to run marketing, for example, if it's the CEO's wheelhouse. That candidate could be extremely skilled, but they'd be a poor fit for COO, given what you need. Or maybe they're an extrovert when you need an inward-facing, analytical COO; or they've always worked in big corporate jobs, but you need someone more entrepreneurial.

SKILLS INTERVIEW

Use the basic criteria—culture fit, behavioral traits, core values, and compatibility with the CEO—to narrow down the candidate pool to four or five strong candidates with the right culture fit. Then give each a skills interview to find out if they have sufficient experience with the core projects that would be on their plate.

Sometimes, the CEO doesn't have the aptitude to do the skills-based interview, such as when the second-in-command needs to oversee engineering or finance because those areas are not the CEO's strengths—the reason for hiring a COO in the first place. In those cases, the CEO has to be honest with themselves and have advisors or department leads interview for the skill components. The danger is that a CEO may otherwise end up hiring a person simply because they like them, and not necessarily because the person has the skills to do the job. Interviewing to hire a COO uses all the same skills that I cover in the people and interviewing sections of my first book, *Double Double*, and my Invest in Your Leaders course. Both have great content on interviewing and should be reviewed by you and anyone assisting in the interviewing process for a COO or any key hires.

TOPGRADING REFERENCES

This isn't a book about interviewing—if you need one, I'd suggest Geoff Smart's book *Who* or Bradford Smart's *Topgrading*—but I want to make a particular point about interviewing.

In the course of your interviews, each candidate is likely to mention ten or so people they've worked with and reported to or who have reported to them. At the end of the second interview, ask them to provide email addresses and phone numbers for at least eight of those ten people. Explain that you're not going to call the three references they provided but may call seven or eight of the ten people they've mentioned.

The A-players will return with all ten, the B-players will give about eight, and the C-players will run away. They're out of there.

At the next interview, spend ninety minutes or a couple of

hours asking what each of those references would say about the candidate. Would they confirm that the candidate lives by the core values? Would they confirm the skills presented? This threat of reference check (TORC) provides the basis for you to ask very probing questions. In that time, you learn a great deal about the true character and skill set of a person. The strong candidates would love it if you called their auxiliary references, while the weak ones won't even show up.

When I do reference checks, they go something like this: "Look, Ben, I'm calling about Bob. I'm thinking of bringing him on as my COO. I know there's some bad stuff in there that I'm going to find out later, but I need you to tell me now what it is. And please don't make me chase you down the street and beat you up with a baseball bat when I find it out later. Tell me the bad shit. I will keep pushing and keep pushing and keep pushing until you tell me the bad stuff." I call up to ten people to do reference checks on key hires, because the day they start, I need to know everything about them. I've worked way too hard to get to this stage to allow somebody to come in whom I don't know enough about. You, too. You are not looking for your A players on Craigslist. You have to poach them. And you have to know them.

KNOW YOUR CANDIDATE IN ADVANCE

Some CEOs—too many—tell me that it takes thirty to ninety days after a person starts working for them to know if they made the right decision. I tell them, "That's because you suck at interviewing."

If you do the interview process properly, you'll know everything there is to know about the person the day they start working for you. There'll be nothing left to learn.

Imagine getting married to someone and waiting to see how the first three months turn out. To know if you should marry someone, you date, you see if you're physically compatible, you ensure you fit together, and then you get married. If you start by getting married and seeing if the rest falls into place, you're taking an enormous risk with your life.

It's the same in business. A three-month trial period is a horrible way to approach hiring, especially for such a pivotal position as a second-in-command. Leaving things up to chance sets you up for failure and is potentially very harmful for your organization. Hiring the wrong senior executive can be incredibly disruptive. It's also very time consuming. If you go through the recruiting and interviewing process, then have the person for three months before you start the process again, you'll have wasted almost a year.

I have recruited and interviewed on a large scale with repeatedly excellent results. At College Pro Painters, we had to go out and get eight hundred brand-new franchisees every year. Between May 1 and August 31, those eight hundred franchisees hired eight thousand painters who were all college students. We went from sixty to nine thousand employees and produced $64 million in revenue in four months. On August 31, all 8,800 kids quit and went back to school. On September 1, we woke up and said, "Oh, shit—we have to do it all again."

And we did. Year after year. I was a part of that very senior leadership team for four years. Fun fact: one of my hires was Kimbal Musk, Elon's brother.

In that scenario, you soon become operationally world-class at recruiting, interviewing, selection, training, and onboarding. In such a short working window, you don't have the luxury of waiting ninety days to see if someone is the right fit. To be perfectly honest, you don't have that luxury in *any* industry. If you interview and hire properly, from a position of knowing who it is you're looking for, you can save yourself a lot of pain.

TAKE IT ON TRUST

It all comes down to trust. Before you hire your new second-in-command, I want you to know so much about them, and be so confident in them, that on the day they start, you'd be happy to give them your master password, your bank account information, and the keys to your house. You'd let them take care of your kids and travel with your spouse for a week.

If that complete, implicit trust isn't there, then don't make an offer. It's as simple as that.

WHAT TO OFFER

I've explained how search firms specialize in filling posts within particular salary ranges, and how salary expectations are so closely linked to job titles, so let's spend a little time on practicalities. What *should* you offer a second-in-command?

The answer depends on where your business is right now, what you need, and how much you can pay. (For guidance on what COOs currently get paid globally, check the survey I mentioned earlier: https://cooalliance.com/salary-survey.) If I wanted to hire the best chief marketing officer in the country, for example, I guess it would be the CMO for Apple. That might be possible—but it would likely cost me $10 million a year. That's not realistic for me...or for most other businesses.

If you run a small, early-stage, venture-capital-funded operation, you're competing with bigger blue-chip names. You'll need to offer equity or a long-term incentive package, because candidates won't risk working with a startup unless there's a big upside.

In some cases, however, it's risky to give out equity, particularly if you've never given it to any other team member. Introducing the practice in order to get the COO you want can open you up to potential conflict, if you've grown a team internally and then give an outsider something they haven't received. Compensation that's poorly thought out really pisses people off. As it should.

SALARY ONLY

My preference is to pay executives a fair salary based on their role and responsibilities, and that's it. I don't think bonuses incentivize strong senior executives to work harder than normal. People will work how they've always worked—hard— so pay them fairly based on the role, and then fire them if they don't meet expectations. Bonus systems are unnecessarily complicated.

Most professional sports teams don't pay bonuses to individual athletes for scoring goals, points, or runs. If the athlete is an offensive player, scoring is their job. Teams recruit good people and expect them to score goals because they're goal-driven players. That's it. It doesn't make sense to hire someone for a base salary and then pay per goal scored.

The same goes for seasoned executives: there's actually some data to show that bonuses demotivate more than they motivate. In Dan Pink's TEDx Talk *The Puzzle of Motivation*, he talks about bonuses not making sense except in true eat-what-you-kill sales roles. Real professionals are already doing their best possible work, so just pay them very fairly for doing it.

Bonuses can also leave people feeling unhappy all year, except for the two weeks when their check is bigger and they spend wildly. It's better to raise their base pay so they can have a somewhat better lifestyle all year long. (Profit-sharing based on outcomes is different from a bonus based on effort, however. It makes sense to include the COO and all senior executives, managers, and so on in profit-sharing structures, if you're putting them in place.)

When you have a solid recruiting process, conduct meaningful interviews, use TORC, and do the proper reference checks, you can feel confident that you're bringing on a great person. In that scenario, you don't need performance-based pay to compensate for a lack of vetting, which is generally what's happening with bonuses.

Title	Male/Female	Company Revenue	# of Employees	Salary	Your Avail. Bonus	Equity
COO	Male	$11,000,000	74	$140,000		None
COO	Female	$11,000,000	21	$60,000	$100,000	None
COO	Male	$11,500,000	140	$155,000		In notes
COO	Male	$12,000,000	80	$250,000	$50,000	1%
COO	Male	$13,000,000	90	$200,000		
CFO/GM	Male	$15,000,000	130	$207,000	$55,000	1%
COO	Male	$15,000,000	95	$200,000	$20,000	2% Sale bonus
COO	Male	$15,000,000	30	$195,000	$36,000	None
COO	Male	$15,000,000	130	$126,000	$50,000	6%
COO	Male	$30,000,000	85	$300,000		6%
COO	Female	$30,000,000	62	$225,000	$75,000	None
VP Ops	Female	$30,000,000	71	$100,000	$60,000	None
COO	Female	$38,000,000	120	$250,000		33.33%
COO	Male	$43,000,000	500+	$260,000	$130,000	Equity increases with growth
Dir Ops	Male	$50,000,000	120	$110,000	$10,000	None
COO	Male	$54,000,000	50	$80,000	$50,000	
VP Ops	Female	$90,000,000	80	$160,000	$60,000	1% equity
VP Ops	Female	$100,000,000	260	$250,000		
SVP Ops	Male	$450,000,000	220	$270,000	$80K-120K*	
COO	Male	$40,000,000	62	$210,000	$65,000	

*Typical range based on net profit of company.

Samples of average compensation per job title/business size

ROLE AND TITLE

As we've discussed, the exact role and title depend on the needs and size of the business. A second-in-command might be titled COO, President, VP of Operations, General Manager, Director of Operations, or Operations Manager. The precise title depends on the responsibilities associated with the job description, the value the role brings to the organization, and what you'll pay for that value.

The bigger the title you give a person, the more it can skew their expectations of their responsibilities, reach, and the accompanying salary. They may also be less inclined to roll up their sleeves and get dirty. Given the role you've outlined and what you can pay, what would you call it? Be cautious with giving out titles that are too big too early, especially COO, because some come with a significant amount of power. Remember that you're not looking for a COO, per se. You're looking for someone to do the work in the job description—be it a COO or not. And if you do give out bigger titles too early, they have no title left to strive for as they grow.

Ginny Lee, COO of Khan Academy, explained how she learned to be less interested in her title than in the work she would be doing: "A business school professor of mine named Jim Collins...said, 'Don't pay attention to the title. Don't pay attention to adjectives that you think you will get your confidence from. Focus on the company, its values, and making sure it's aligned with your own values.'"

Whatever title you land on, the org chart needs to clarify roles, responsibilities, and reporting structure. If IT and finance report to the COO, can the COO just show up at their meetings? If marketing reports to the second-in-command, is it appropriate for the COO to drop in unannounced? Of course, as a leader, you *can*, but sitting in different business areas and meetings requires a certain finesse, especially when those people don't report directly to you.

The COO might be responsible for aligning, growing, and understanding all parts of the organization, but they also need to respect the various area leaders and avoid stepping on their toes or getting in their way. Having a clear org chart sets expectations, after which you can decide when or whether it is ever appropriate to deviate from the structure. Just because the COO *can* show up doesn't mean they should, because it can have unintended consequences. Their focus should be on removing obstacles for people rather than bossing them around.

PART 3

WORKING WITH A COO

CHAPTER 7

ONBOARDING

"The COO Alliance would have been extremely helpful for me to have when I was first put into my position. There is no other individual in the company that understands exactly what I do and what it all entails, not even the CEO. I have enjoyed being able to utilize others in the COO Alliance the way I do now, and I can only imagine how much more I could have learned and implemented right off the bat."

—ASHLEY WIEDERHOEFT, COO ALLIANCE
MEMBER AND ASSISTANT VICE PRESIDENT
AT GREAT PLAINS TRANSPORTATION

A new COO arrives in a business like a boulder being dropped into a pond. There are ripples everywhere. Some employees will feel frustrated because they'll wish they'd been given the job, and others will feel excited to report to this new person and grow their careers. Some suppliers won't want to start a relationship with a new contact, while others will appreciate the support and enhanced systems.

Done well, the COO's arrival could free up the CEO to galvanize the company culture as the chief energizing officer or to focus on whatever they've identified as their Unique Abilities. Done badly, the ripples create disruption throughout the business.

If you've hired the right person and onboard them well, the COO will settle in perfectly. If you rush to get them into the business without an intentional onboarding process, however, you run the risk of any CEO's greatest nightmare: unintended consequences.

The CEO doesn't get to step back the day a COO arrives. Even if that's the ultimate aim, the CEO has a responsibility to remain engaged to ensure any transition is successful.

Your business is your child. Imagine if one parent left the other to raise the kids and didn't check back for six months. Your kids are going to get pissed at you for being absent, and you might realize that they've drifted off the course you would have chosen. But you can't say shit because you weren't around.

Raising a company is the same as raising kids. The parents need to be involved.

FIRST NINETY DAYS

Before your COO ever starts, you need a clear onboarding plan for their first ninety days and beyond. Their first priority is to learn about the history and culture of the company, the core values, how you got where you are, the team dynamics, the people, the industry, the customers, the suppliers, and the "operating manual" of how to deal with you and with each of the others on the leadership team.

They have a lot to take onboard, but they need that foundation in place before they start making decisions. Don't expect them to do too much in the first few weeks. In fact, you should positively discourage them from taking action. Don't make the mistake of handing over the reins too early. That will only screw up the transition.

I divide onboarding of senior leaders into three parts:

- **Month 1.** This period is about understanding; everyone should understand that the COO isn't making any decisions at this stage. They simply observe, sit in on meetings, get to know people, and take notes. Lots of notes. I tell new hires to keep a notebook with a running list of all their ideas and observations regarding what they'd like to do.
- **Month 2.** The next period is about looking for opportunities to change systems and processes, and potentially people. The COO should go back and reassess or stress-test previous ideas in their notebook to see if they're still relevant. They can dig in with the team regarding their observations and assumptions to see if they have an accurate picture.
- **Month 3.** After two months of bedding in, the COO can start making changes based on everything they have learned. This is when they can start executing because the best apparent course of action will have changed as they've learned more about the details, dynamics, and people.

It's dangerous to execute on too much too early, because a new hire can't have the necessary information and insights. It can be frustrating for COOs to restrain themselves, given that they've usually been hired to make changes and will want to get going, but what seems to make sense in the first week can look very different three weeks later. Coming out swinging makes everyone nervous and can damage important relationships in the long- term.

Any changes should flow from observation and tested hypotheses. If the COO thinks people need to be swapped out for new personnel, they should first understand what led to the current configuration. They should identify gaps. COOs often want to recruit by bringing others with them, but they first need to get to know and understand the existing team to establish a mutually positive working relationship.

In the early stage, the CEO should also stay relatively hands-off and give the COO room to observe. As long as they are purely observing and not trying to execute, there's little concern about having them sit in on any meeting they want, taking people to lunch or coffee, conducting informational interviews across the organization, attending functional and project meetings, and generally riding shotgun in as many areas of the business as possible.

Maybe the COO notices fifteen different areas for improvement. Before acting, they should rank their improvement ideas by greatest impact to create a firm foundation for their changes. If they simply start changing things, the effort will be scattered. After sixty days, they'll have a firm enough understanding to build out a project map based on their observations and can begin executing in an organized, orderly fashion. It's slowing down to go fast or learning to walk before they can run.

Sean Magennis, President and COO of YPO (Young Presidents Organization), describes the dynamic in this way:

> I would not rush any type of communication or interaction with key employees. I've learned to take time. What happens with that is you lose connectivity and you don't establish relationships. My brother uses an interesting illustration. He says, "You've got to make deposits in order to make withdrawals." I think of that statement ten times a week. The more you put into individuals, the more you'll be able to have them respect, trust, or forgive you.

Whether the COO needs permission from the CEO to take action depends on the actual role and responsibilities, but the aim of the onboarding process is to get buy-in from the team. In the movie *Taps*, Timothy Hutton plays a top military cadet whose father is an army general. The general tells his son that the men will respect a title, but they also need to respect the individual who holds it.

In business, people will respect a COO's authority by virtue of their being the COO—but those people still need to respect the individual behind the desk, as well. It takes at least thirty to sixty days to achieve that by building trust and working relationships. That way, when the COO starts to make decisions, they don't piss people off. If they start acting too early, without the full view of the team, they'll create ripple effects, backchannel communication, or avoidable tension.

HITTING EVERY BENCHMARK

Onboarding is finished when the COO has met every benchmark in the process. If I were the CEO, I'd want them to meet one-on-one with every VP and Director, have lunch or coffee with each of them, sit in on each of the business area meetings to observe, sit in on some job interviews to observe, review the last ninety days' project plan, fully understand the Vivid Vision, talk to suppliers and customers, understand the whole sales cycle, go through the trainings other staff go through, and be fully up to speed.

I've written five books, and new employees read all of them—in addition to going through my Invest in Your Leaders course—as part of the onboarding process. If your company has written books or offers courses, new hires should read them and attend them.

Well-executed onboarding builds trust and understanding with teams before the COO fully takes over direction of projects. In *Five Dysfunctions of a Team*, Pat Lencioni talks about artificial harmony and the absence of trust. If you can build good harmony with others, and a foundation of trust and respect in which you know people's roles and responsibilities and what's happening in their personal lives, you will have a strong foundation to get more work done later.

CEOs have a cheerleading component to their role. If the COO is also a cheerleader but hasn't developed a level of trust and understanding with the team, their cheerleading can come off as patronizing or misplaced. Cheerleading should focus on those of a person's activities that require cheering on. If the COO cheerleads a function that everyone has already mastered, it seems tone-deaf.

The incoming COO should read the résumé of every single person on the leadership team to get to know them and understand what they're doing and have done. They should look at everyone's LinkedIn and social media profiles, as well.

The COO needs to take the time to truly understand the organization and not jump to conclusions; understand the people and relationships so they don't cause unnecessary ripple effects; and build trust so people can feel secure under their leadership and come to them with problems. Moving too quickly with decisions causes damage.

There's no need to rush. At the start, it's better to let something continue at 70 percent efficiency than to make a situation worse.

The COO will learn the ropes as they go. Once they have more clarity, they can make decisions with confidence. The team will align behind them and support them. If they make decisions too quickly, even if they're making the right decisions, they jeopardize communication and the foundational security of the team.

OPERATING MANUAL

When you buy a TV, Sonos, iPhone, or any other piece of electronic equipment, you get an operating manual. Rippling COO Matt MacInnis created an operating manual for himself that he gives to every employee. (You can read the full text in this book's Appendix.) If he starts in a new company, he gives it to the entire company. When new employees join the company and start reporting to him as COO, he sends it to them.

It summarizes how he operates, how he ticks, what drives him crazy, what pisses him off, what turns him on, and how he makes decisions. His interview with me on the *Second in Command* podcast outlined his process beautifully.

Onboarding serves to bring people into the company in the most efficient way, get them up to speed, make them feel comfortable and ready to do their job, and make others feel good about working with them—without causing too much disruption. Matt's operating manual helps prevent some of the ripple effects of dropping the boulder into the middle of the organization's pond.

Can you imagine if everyone on the team created their own operating manual so that they all knew how to work with each other?

A COO wants to maintain their authority while also remaining approachable. People need to understand the COO and get up to speed as quickly as possible, getting to know each other so they can hit the ground running with sufficient trust and respect. Explicitly sharing guidelines for engaging with the COO is a great way to make sure everyone is on the same page.

COO ALLIANCE

Onboarding a COO gets them into the organization, but things don't stop there. No CEO can afford to let their COO stop growing their skills. Some COOs read thought leadership books constantly, taking notes and comparing them with colleagues. Others employ coaches. Whitney Bouck, COO of Hello Sign, would advise young COOs, "Be opportunistic, build your network, and keep looking for new opportunities to learn. Surround yourself with people who can teach you things. Those opportunities will present themselves and teach you what you love to do—and therefore what you're best at."

I started the COO Alliance because no other strong networks for COOs even exist. And I strongly believe that traditional business models teach the wrong person how to grow a company. We shouldn't be teaching the CEO how to grow the business, build teams, run meetings, plan, and market. As a CEO, you should know *about* those areas; but the COO should receive the training and build the skills needed to actually handle them for you. Entrepreneurial CEOs tend to tune out after five minutes, whereas the COO will stay engaged for an entire training course. They actually give a shit. And they need to.

The COO Alliance filled a gap in the business world: a thought leadership group exclusively for seconds in command, with membership limited to those working for an organization making at least $5 million in revenue. It doesn't matter whether people's title is Director of Operations, GM, or COO; these are essentially the people who would be running the company if the CEO weren't there.

Like CEO, COO can be a lonely job—but at the COO Alliance, COOs can talk to their peers. We're the world's leading community for seconds in command, connecting them with ops-minded professionals to learn new strategies and develop revenue-generating ideas with some of the best business experts in the world.

It's a trusted community of executives from seventeen countries, as of the time of this writing. Members join a vetted peer group of COOs who speak their language, and the COO Alliance gives them the tools and connections they need to grow themselves and their business.

We also give members a 10X Guarantee. After completing their annual membership, if they don't get ten times the value of their investment back in savings or potential profits, we give them their money back—no questions asked, no catch. All we ask is that they jump in with both feet, actively participate, and give it a genuine go.

It's a true alliance. COOs must be willing to share, not just to take others' ideas. We only look for members who want to contribute and grow in equal measure. They need a willingness to be vulnerable and to help others.

For CEOs, getting their COO involved with the COO Alliance is hugely powerful. It gives them an unfair advantage, because it gives their COO access to resources that other companies don't have.

BROADENING PERSPECTIVE AND RECOGNIZING COMMONALITY

The CEO and COO share the same box, and—like the CEO—the COO often doesn't see outside the box unless they make an effort to expand their horizons. Imagine two executives tasked with clear-cutting a forest. They might be cutting down all the trees perfectly—but it's only when they climb to the top of the tallest tree that they realize they're cutting in the wrong forest.

That's why it's so important to have a larger perspective about the role and the business landscape than what happens within your own C-suite. It's hard to get that perspective from anywhere—but belonging to the COO Alliance can provide it.

COO Alliance members range in age from twenty-six to sixty-two, and at the time of this writing, 41 percent of our members are women.

COO is a vastly varied role, but the COO Alliance community has revealed commonalities across the diversity. First, members learn that everyone has imposter syndrome and feels like they're doing the biggest thing they've ever done. They all feel a little bit nervous that they might screw up.

That realization alone—that everyone is in the same boat—helps give members confidence to temper the imposter syndrome and create a stronger foundation for their work. They also gain connections with a network of peers to go to with questions and concerns, which makes them feel less alone and helps them solve problems. They realize they don't have to know how to do everything, just who could solve a problem. Members leverage our Slack work group to ask questions and share resources.

Another commonality among many COOs is thinking that their CEO or visionary is a little bit crazy (or a lot crazy). That's not a negative judgment—most of our members are in awe of the vision and energy of their CEO—but an acknowledgment that knowing how to leverage an unconventional CEO requires special support. COOs in the alliance learn to accept that they're constitutionally different from their entrepreneurial CEOs—and that it's okay and normal to have that difference.

COOs also learn they need to outsource more, and the network's shared resource pool can help them find the best freelancers and shortcuts. Many of them use the executive search firms and Fractional CFOs and CMOs I recommend. At the time of this writing, three or four are working with the same M&A group to help them sell the company.

Despite all its members having different roles, titles, and organizations, the COO Alliance transcends the differences. They learn there is no one system they can use to grow their company. It's not like the recipe for a Manhattan cocktail—there's no recipe you can Google for how to grow a company. Our members learn about everyone's systems and might pick up on two or three different ideas and use them to make something better for themselves.

I call it "ideas having sex."

KEEP BRINGING IN NEW IDEAS

New ideas come into an organization in multiple ways. Often, they come through the CEO, because CEOs tend to belong to mastermind communities and entrepreneurial organizations where they have the greatest exposure to best practices and thought leadership.

Because the COO is in charge of figuring out how to make it all happen, they should also be looking for new tools and resources to grow the skills of the people. They should be reading books, looking for courses and mentoring opportunities for their team, and continuing to find new systems to incorporate best practices.

Just as you belong to networking and mastermind groups, make sure you get your COO into a mastermind group like COO Alliance, as well, so that they're also building a network. The COO doesn't have to know how to do everything, but they do have to know how to find the answers they need—and the best place to start is with a dedicated sharing community.

COO COACHING

To CEOs who don't like execution and can barely listen to an hour-long talk without losing interest, a COO is something of a miracle: a one-person band who can play every instrument in the business at the same time. But that multitasking can be deceptive. Your second-in-command has strengths and weaknesses—and your job is to identify their Unique Abilities and coach them to become world-class and to inject rocket fuel into your organization.

But remember: you coach what they're good at. If they suck at something, screw it. They can delegate to someone else who's good at it.

There is no critical mass of COO-specific coaches, so coaching for COOs tends to come from CEO coaches who are former seasoned senior executives and who concentrate on different aspects: skills, mindset, leadership, or a specific domain such as interviewing or finance.

Over time, best practices in some areas remain fairly stable, but others shift rapidly and represent logical areas for coaching. The CEO's vision has a longer trajectory, but the COO needs to respond to externals that can be extremely trying: a pandemic, a mass resignation, or another dynamic. Marketing and technology are constantly changing. Automation, optimization, offshoring, outsourcing, and even running effective meetings in hybrid work situations can present challenges and areas for growth.

Even though I've always been a people person, I benefited from coaching around maintaining relationships. I used to take criticism way too personally. I was okay with giving others constructive criticism but needed to improve how I received it. Through coaching and mentoring from the likes of Joan Mara and Greg Johnson, I improved my ability to maintain openness, respect, and mutual affinity with employees. I had monthly calls with Greg and then met with him in person every quarter, and that deep work paid off in my role at building teams.

Greg was very operational—and engineering-, enterprise-, and scale-focused—but that's not what I needed from him. What I needed was pure leadership development, removing blind spots and showing me how a real leader of a real company works. Helping me with my freaking email overload. I was getting two hundred emails a day, and I thought that was a lot, but he was getting thousands a day. How did he deal with that?

When I was with College Pro Painters, the leaders' skill set was exemplary because the company invested time in growing the soft skills of the leadership team to a level not ordinarily seen in business. Other companies I've worked with had leaders with strong functional skills but little cross-training, so there were inconsistencies in how they delegated, dealt with conflict, coached, and so on.

I launched the Invest in Your Leaders course for COOs, and even key managers, because leaders need to know how to grow people's skills and confidence as they climb the ladder within an organization. COOs should continually assess the best ways to facilitate that growth in all business areas.

COO SURVEY

When determining coaching needs, COO Alliance's COO Survey can help CEOs rate their COOs, or it can help COOs rate themselves. I learned this scorecard concept from Dan Sullivan's awesome Strategic Coach program, which I believe all entrepreneurs need to join. Regarding this COO Scorecard, it's important to start from the understanding that no one's perfect. No matter how skilled we are at our role, we all have room to grow. As Ray Kroc, who built McDonald's, put it, "When you're green, you're growing. When you're ripe, you're rotting."

This survey provides a good starting point to think about that growth and how to become better in a role.

Below are a few of the areas covered on the COO Survey showing the possibilities COOs have for growing in their capabilities. Effective COOs rate seven and above, and exemplary COOs rate ten and above in these areas. You can take the full assessment to rate your COO at https://cooalliance. com/ceo-survey/.

There's also a survey for COOs to rate themselves and identify areas where they could improve—by reading, coaching, or signing up to the COO Alliance. They can find it here: https:// cooalliance.com/survey/.

Mindsets	1	2	3	4	5	6	7	8	9	10	11	12	Score
1 Vision— Aligned with CEO	You have an idea what each other wants. You're always arguing or there is frustration over which direction to go.			You have occasional problems. Some disagreements in front of employees. You second-guess priorities of others on the team.			You seem to be on the same page. There are the occasional bumps in the road. Your team sees you as aligned.			You have complete trust due to being on the same page. You refer back to the Vivid Vision frequently. You share the vision frequently with employees, customers and suppliers.			
2 Strategic Plan in Place	You have no plan. You're on different pages. Business areas are confused or frustrated. No expenses are planned for. You feel like you're winging it.			You have an okay plan on paper. Rarely looked at. Not sure it's even accurate any more. Better than you used to be, though.			Your plan is in writing. It's reviewed quarterly. Most people know the details of it. You have a fairly ad-hoc process for reviewing it.			Your plan is in Asana (or similar) and is referred to weekly by the leadership team. Cross departmental dependencies are considered. You consider Money, People & Time Requirements.			
3 People Systems— Recruiting, Interviewing & Hiring	You have Cs and Bs working for you. No one is trained in interviewing. You use Craigslist mostly for job postings. People quit frequently.			Your people are mostly good. You promote from within. It's a hard labor market to find good people, but you do okay.			You have solid Bs on the team. Some basic interviewing skills internally. Hopefully, your Cs will improve or quit. Occasionally your team does reference checks on new hires.			You do in-person 360 group feedback reviews. You Top Grade all staff every six months. A Virtual Bench is in place. Everyone is trained & certified in Interviewing.			
4 Meetings	You run unorganized meetings and hate attending them. You have no idea how to run effective meetings. You're not sure what meetings to even have.			You haven't been trained on running meetings, nor have employees. However they're pretty good. Not sure what to do differently or how to run them better.			You run them pretty well. And have some fixed meeting rhythms. Some casual training around how to run them or participate in them.			Your employees have read *Meetings Suck*. No time is wasted. Strong focus on outputs. They are fun and high impact. People take pride in opting out.			

Mindsets	1	2	3	4	5	6	7	8	9	10	11	12	Score
5 Financial	You have no budget to work from. Financial statements are occasionally produced, often with mistakes. And you're not even sure what to look at when you have them.			Your numbers are okay but you know there are mistakes. Financials aren't timely. You're not sure what to look at or how to read financials.			Your financials are timely and mostly accurate. Some solid financial KPIs are reviewed regularly. Cash flow is good.			You have rolling past & future 12-month budgets. You have a good eye on cash flow. Open book financials for all employees.			
6 Skills to Do the Job of COO	You have no idea where you stack up or how to improve. You feel stuck, overwhelmed & useless at times. You're way over your head. And have no idea where to turn.			You worry you will get replaced or made redundant. Thought you were smart until now. You know that you have lots to learn, but where to start?			You turn to books for learning. You have sporadic training sessions in-house. You attend the occasional conferences or courses. You don't have a formal growth plan.			You're always growing as a leader. You focus your learning on your 6- to 12-month objectives. You're a part of masterminds and book clubs.			
7 Mentors	You feel alone. No one to regularly turn to. No idea where to actually go for help or what you should start learning.			You are not sure where to turn for help. You don't think you can find anyone to help you. How much will it even cost?			You turn to others occasionally. You know where you need to improve. And you feel supported in your role.			You have a TOP 50 list of mentors that you call on regularly. You leverage the wisdom of the crowd. You will reach out to leaders you read about in the media for advice.			
8 Culture	You could describe your culture as "Beige." You "don't really have a culture." Never given it much thought. Isn't culture for tech companies.			Your culture is pretty good. No one really complains that much. You're sure where you stack up against other companies. Lots to improve on.			Your people are happy working with you. No one complains. You have lots of perks. Recruiting new hires isn't that hard.			You have an award-winning culture. You leverage tools like TINYpulse, and have strong Glass Door ratings. It's easy to recruit A players.			
Scorecard													

CAPABILITY 1: VISION ALIGNMENT

- The first area of the scorecard rates COOs on how aligned they are with the CEO's vision.
- In poorly run companies, it's not clear whether the COO knows what the CEO wants. You're always arguing, or there is frustration over which direction to go.
- In marginally better-run companies, there are occasional problems between the CEO and COO regarding vision. You may have disagreements over direction in front of employees. The COO does not know how to prioritize work to hit the vision. Sometimes, the COO seems to be on the same page as the CEO. There are occasional bumps in the road, but the team sees you as aligned.
- In the best run companies, the COO and CEO have complete trust in each other because they are on the same page. The COO refers to the CEO's Vivid Vision frequently, and employees, customers, and suppliers also understand that vision.

In the case of vision alignment, when the COO doesn't know what the CEO wants to do or where the company is going, it's often because the CEO has never shared that vision. Your responsibility as a CEO is to sit down with the COO and spell it out.

My Vivid Vision for the COO Alliance, for example, is a four-page description of the company's trajectory, projected three years into the future. Here it is:

COO ALLIANCE: 025 VIVID VISION

The following is our COO Alliance 2025 Vivid Vision. Creating a Vivid Vision brings the future into the present, so everyone has clarity on what we're building now. It's a detailed overview of what the COO Alliance will look like, act like, and feel like three years out—by December 31, 2025. Sharing it with others helps it become reality!

OUR MEMBERS

The COO Alliance is the only truly global network of its kind in the *world* for those who are second-in-command. The quality of our members continues to grow. Our average member is doing upward of $50 million with 75–7,500 employees. And our minimum criteria for membership is $5 million in revenue or capital raised. We have a pure Facebook-only group for seconds in command where we allow smaller companies doing a minimum of $1 million to join. All full-time 500 COO Alliance members are active participants with a strong desire to learn, a willingness to share, and the vulnerability to never be the smartest person in the room.

They recognize that their growth as COOs comes from learning from each other, conversations with peers, and teaching COOs at smaller companies. Our online-only membership has 5,000 members with access to recorded content and their own private Facebook group. Through monthly live Q&As via Zoom meetings with other members and myself, they receive hands-on, personal attention to support them with their challenges and celebrate their successes so they can continue to grow themselves and their companies.

WHAT IT LOOKS LIKE

We host online events every month, and members can also elect to attend any of our two optional in-person events as well. Our members interact with each other between meetings—via our COO Alliance Portal, our private Slack channel, and Zoom—to continue supporting each other in their growth.

LOCATION

Our twelve monthly global events are held via Zoom. Our two annual in-person events are held at amazing properties in sunny Scottsdale, Arizona; Dubai; Europe; and the mountainous ocean-side city of Vancouver, Canada. I host opening night cocktail parties at amazing locations. The perfect weather allows us to do many of our breakout sessions and meals outdoors, and we incorporate morning yoga, bike rides, hikes, and fun into all our events.

WORLD-CLASS CONTENT

The content from the COO Alliance events comes in a variety of forms:

- member-to-member learning breakouts
- small group workshops
- informal time
- ten-minute talks given by members on their own areas of expertise
- expert guest speakers who come in to share with us

We operate the meetings in a confidential environment that allows everyone to feel comfortable in truly sharing and opening up with each other. Members give presentations to the group on areas where they feel stuck, and they receive in-depth feedback and experience- sharing from other members. We work through a variety of forms, worksheets, and exercises to encourage members to be introspective, grow themselves as leaders, and grow their companies' revenue, profitability, customer engagement, and employee culture.

We have amazingly deep discussions as a group at all events. And we frequently share tips for members in their private Slack group, as well as upload ten-minute talks into our private Members app so they can share the content with their company's employees and never miss a beat. Members also share video content with their company's employees. We also share all our 450-plus *Second in Command* podcasts with members, and frequently interview their companies on the podcast as well. This gives them a unique opportunity to showcase their expertise, broaden exposure, achieve influencer status, and increase traffic to their business.

The content from the COO Alliance events covers a variety of core topics:

- CEO/COO Relationship: Building an Unbreakable Bond Amongst Rapid Change
- Strategic Thinking and Planning: Gaining Clarity Around Vision
- Operations and Execution: Transforming Ideas into Reality
- People and Processes: Recruiting, Interviewing, Selection, Top-grading, Onboarding, Handcuffing A-Players, and Offboarding
- World-Class Culture: Cultivating an Amazing Workplace Culture That Attracts Employees and Clients Like a Magnet
- Technology Tools: Leveraging and Streamlining People and Processes

- Leadership and Skill Development: Increasing Confidence and Capabilities
- Meetings That Don't Suck: Running Highly Effective, Impactful Meetings
- Coaching and Delegation: Attracting and Growing a Unique Ability Team
- and more...

CONNECT AND RECHARGE

At all monthly events, we members really get to know each other. And we often have super fun social components. At each in-person event, we do a fun activity with the group such as Top Golf, Escape Rooms, Camelback hikes, cycling, golf, morning runs, or yoga. This serves as a reminder to disconnect and have some fun, in addition to providing an opportunity to connect with each other on a deeper level outside the meeting space.

BENEFITS AND COMMUNITY

Since day one, we've told members that after a year of attending, they'll leave with ideas that are worth 10X their investment in either savings or new revenue, or we give them their money back. No one has ever taken us up on it. Our Member NPS hovers around 70 percent at each event. We have more than fifty accountability groups, with 75 percent of our members participating, so now members push each other throughout the year to put their ideas into action. They finally feel like they have "their tribe" to learn from. Members get value from working one-on-one with me at these events, but they find the greatest advantage in learning from each other. Plus, they no longer need to waste their time attending CEO events where there is little information targeted specifically to them. This is their tribe.

THE CULTURE

Members greatly appreciate the time to slow down, think, plan, and work on both themselves and their company without the day-to-day distractions of business. Our onsite film and audio crews capture content throughout all the meetings for offline and online COO Alliance members to learn from and review between events. The culture we're building in this mastermind is one of focused personal and business growth. We're all in this to grow ourselves and our companies in an open and trusting environment. We've created a culture where we can be vulnerable with each other and comfortably share our fears, insecurities, weaknesses, dreams, desires, and goals. And we finally feel like we have support from our peers for the first time. As COOs, we aren't here to goof off, but we still have fun while we work. We assist each other with our growth initiatives between meetings, providing an extra level of accountability and support.

MARKETING

We've done a great job marketing the COO Alliance to find new members. All of our leads go into a sales funnel so that we can not only market to potential members, but also add value to them as COOs before and after they join. Our website shows the statistics of current member companies and includes profiles of members and their raving testimonials. We have marketing set up on autopilot through Facebook, other social media platforms, magazine ads, direct mail, and LinkedIn. And we have re-targeting in place so that prospects consistently see us even before they've decided to join.

Our *Second in Command* podcast and magazine columns build credibility, and we leverage that into signing up stronger and stronger members and companies into the COO Alliance. We're getting a ton of exposure in the press about the program, our members, and our team. Referrals from CEOs encouraging each other to have their COOs join account for 30 percent of our signed new members.

OUR TEAM

We're a fast-growing, high-energy team of self-starters and doers, with a high level of passion for and pride in our mission. Our COO handles all the key parts of the company, allowing everyone to focus on their areas of Unique Ability. We have fantastic people in place to head up Marketing, Sales, Social Media, Operations, Technology, and Finance. We still leverage freelancers globally, too. We have productive and fun team meetings to align everyone quarterly, monthly, and weekly. Our dashboards keep us focused on the critical areas of the business so we continue to attract new members, curate world-class content, and help millions of COOs grow their people, culture, and profits.

When people read that Vivid Vision, they're completely clear on what I'm building.

Most CEOs have never clarified their vision with their employees and internal leaders. There might be a mission statement or a one-sentence direction, but not enough information for everyone involved to know what the company will look, act, and feel like three years into the future.

Sharing your Vivid Vision with your COO is no different from the collaboration required of a couple raising a family. If you don't discuss and coordinate your actions, you're guaranteed to have miscommunications. If you plan a family vacation but don't agree on what you'll do, then one person might envision lying by the pool while the other envisions engaging in activities all day, every day. Conflict and disorganization will ensue.

CEOs often fall into the trap of thinking the COO is always able to be a mind reader. For a COO to execute effectively, they need to have a strategic plan in place to hit the CEO's vision. Clarity and shared mission allows you to have a yin and yang partnership. You can't wing it and expect positive results.

CAPABILITY 3: SYSTEMS FOR RECRUITING, INTERVIEWING, AND HIRING

- This capability rates COOs on the extent that they have established systems for recruiting, interviewing, and hiring.
- Poorly run companies and bad COOs employ only C- and B-level talent. Managers are not trained in interviewing, and they use Craigslist for most job postings. Employees frequently quit.
- Marginally better-run companies and COOs always promote from within and feel like it's a hard labor market to find good people.
- Things start improving when the COO ensures your company has solid Bs on the team. Managers have some basic interviewing skills. You're hopeful that your Cs will improve or quit. The COO and managers occasionally do reference checks on new hires.
- The best COOs do in-person 360 group feedback reviews, topgrade all staff every six months, and have a virtual

bench of hires in place. They also make sure all managers are trained and certified in interviewing. And they've likely put all their managers through the Invest in Your Leaders course for self-guided skills training.

In most companies, it's common for the CEO to delegate hiring to the COO, and the COO must do the hiring for roles within the business areas reporting to them. To maintain clear communication, the COO needs to ensure there are recruiting, interviewing, hiring, and onboarding systems in place for the whole company.

Such systems serve as guardrails so particular business areas don't veer off-course in hiring people who clash with the culture. Cross-departmental interviews can facilitate hiring better people. Staffing plans allow the finance team to plan budgets. It's also one of the core modules in my Invest in Your Leaders course. In fact, it's critical that any managers doing any interviewing go through this content to avoid making hiring mistakes.

CAPABILITY 5: FINANCIAL SYSTEMS

- This part of the scorecard rates COOs on the financial systems they have established to stay in sync with the CEO's goals, and to ensure the leadership team has the data needed to make planning decisions for growth.
- Poorly run companies have no budget to work from. Their financial statements are produced occasionally but not regularly. The COO isn't even sure what to look at when they have them.
- Middle-ranking companies may have a rough company

budget that shows the numbers are okay, but the COO or CEO worries there are mistakes. Financials aren't timely. And the COO isn't sure how to read them. Sometimes company financials are timely and accurate, and cash flow is good. The COO might occasionally review the financial KPls.

- In better-run companies, the COO has rolling past and future twelve-month budgets produced to manage by. The CEO and COO have a good eye on cash flow. And the COO, with the CFO, manages open-book financials for all employees.

Some CEOs want to keep a tighter handle on financials, but the COO must have access to all the financial information (both restrictions and opportunities) in order to make strategic decisions in the best interest of the company—including which hires they can make, which projects to initiate, and how to continue making progress toward the CEO's overall vision.

The only time there might not be full information-sharing would be in the very early initial stages if you're thinking of selling the company.

CAPABILITY 6: COO SKILLSET

- This capability reflects how a COO stacks up at possessing and improving the skills for the job.
- Poorly performing COOs have no idea how they compare to other COOs; and nor do they know how to improve. At times, the COO feels stuck, overwhelmed, and useless— in way over their head and with no idea where to turn. Many COOs in this category worry they will get replaced

or made redundant. They thought they were smart until now. They know that they have a lot to learn but aren't sure where to start.

- The next rung of COOs sometimes turn to books for learning, have sporadic training sessions in-house, and attend occasional conferences or courses. But often, this COO does not have a formal personal growth plan.

- The best COOs are always growing as leaders and focus their learning on six- to twelve-month objectives. The COO is part of a mastermind group like the COO Alliance, and they're constantly improving on their skills. They see growth as an opportunity for themselves.

The goal of any leader is to grow their people. The more we focus on growing people, the more they'll grow the company. If you have mutual trust, alignment, and excitement about the vision, then you can feel confident your COO will continue using their growth in service of your company rather than looking elsewhere.

Of course, even when you have an effective COO in place, it's essential to keep working on your own growth, as well. I've frequently seen CEOs make the mistake of abdicating responsibility once they install a COO. You want to avoid the situation of handing over too much responsibility, especially before fully vetting and training someone. At the end of the day, it's still your company. The results rest on your choices.

CHAPTER 8

WORKING TOGETHER

"We quickly found our strengths and weaknesses and stayed true to doing what we both were strong at. Of course, we are still ever-changing and...may develop new strengths or start to gravitate away from other things. In those situations...we shift and find the solution based on our own needs."

—RACHEL PACHIVAS, COO ALLIANCE MEMBER
AND COO OF ANNMARIE SKIN CARE

You've done the work. You've figured out the kind of COO you need, you've gone through a recruitment and interviewing process that has led you to the right person, and you've onboarded them into the organization. Now there's one more part of the process you still have to figure out. How will you and your new second-in-command work best together to achieve everything you want for the company?

The key is to take an intentional approach, so start by revisiting all the information you have gathered during the interview process about what the COO is like. Use that information to start building healthy communication and strong trust from the beginning, which is particularly important if other members of the leadership team feel they've lost power to the COO. Engage in trust exercises so you're both okay with telling the truth all the time.

- Open up to each other about your past failures.
- Teach each other skills that you're strong in.
- Walk each other through your Kolbe, DISC or Strengths-finder profiles—focusing on your weaknesses.
- Tell each other about your upbringing.
- Have each team member answer five questions about their personal lives. Sample questions include your hometown, first job, worst job, number of siblings, greatest fear, and something that nobody else knows about you.

Everyone, including all C-level executives, needs to be on the same page about the different roles and responsibilities of the CEO and COO. You can only avoid stepping on each other's toes if everyone in the company knows who to contact for what, who makes which decisions, and who is and isn't involved in different areas. There may be areas the COO is responsible for that used to fall under the purview of other executives, so make sure people have familiarity with the new org chart and chain of command. Because the COO role is company-specific, everything must be spelled out, including how you'll measure the COO's success.

At the same time, the CEO needs to feel good about their own new role and responsibilities after handing off some of what they used to do. Once the COO finishes onboarding, the CEO will not have all the information on every subject anymore, so it's important to recognize where your role ends and the COO's begins, as well as when you both need to confer before making a decision.

Without full clarity and commitment to the new structure, I've seen CEOs start meddling in the COO's responsibilities almost straightaway, especially if they are areas the CEO used to love working on but that are a better fit for the COO. This kind of meddling has a negative impact on productivity and damages trust in the relationship.

You need to have explicit discussions about who deals with what. You also need to involve the leadership team so that everyone is on board with the new path forward. The COO won't make all the decisions in a business area from day one; a gradual transition will likely allow you to feel comfortable with the new arrangement. Maybe you both attend certain meetings or phone calls at first, and then you gradually phase yourself out and make it clear when employees should no longer go to you with questions on that topic.

If everyone continues coming to you with questions, and you engage, it will inevitably end up minimizing the COO and creating triangulation and miscommunication. Lack of coordination between the two of you will lead to unnecessary complexity and left-hand/right-hand issues.

DIVIDE AND CONQUER

Look at everything that needs to get done and decide who should invest their time and energy in each item. Who is the best fit for each type of meeting, the different customer and supplier relationships, and every other business area? You might not hand off everything to the COO at once, but you can gradually divide the responsibilities over time. If you have twelve core suppliers, nine might start reporting to the COO right away, whereas the other three will require more onboarding and the opportunity to shift the relationship. That division will depend on your own UAs, preferences, and bandwidth. Whatever you decide, you're looking for clarity regarding what is on each person's plate.

Jen Leech—President, COO, and cofounder of Truss—describes how she and her CEO defined their domains:

> We each wrote down what accountabilities we were holding and what we loved and hated most about our work. Then we looked for patterns. I took the work that required detailed execution (e.g., Finance) and policy management (e.g., People and Culture), and he took the work that involved developing external relationships and public persona (e.g., Sales and Marketing).

> At 1-800-GOT-JUNK?, Brian had great relationships with the first twelve franchise partners. When I came in as the COO, I said we needed to start encouraging those partners to come to me. We needed to build our own relationships and trust, and they needed to know that I was capable, and that Brian didn't always have all the information on what we were doing anymore. We intentionally built a communication path to keep each other on the same page, which also required Brian to trust me. It wasn't always easy. But we worked at it.

> We needed to act like Navy SEALs: if we ran into a hostile sit-

uation, we had to trust that each of us had our own side of the room covered. We couldn't second-guess the other person or check to make sure they were doing their job. In combat, that kind of distraction gets people killed—and in business it loses clients and productivity. Clarity around roles and responsibilities is key to success.

SPOTLIGHT: MAKE EACH OTHER LOOK GOOD

The CEO and COO need to act in front of others like parents around their kids. It's Dad's job to make Mom look good, and vice versa. Parents can fight behind the scenes, but not in front of the kids. The COO's job is to make the CEO iconic. The CEO rolls out the good news. The COO rolls out the bad news and owns the tough decisions. In turn, it's the CEO's job to shine the spotlight on the COO internally to explain why they need to make those difficult calls. In those kinds of situations, the COO needs the full support of the CEO.

COO Alliance member Hunter McMahon of iDiscovery Solutions describes this dynamic with his CEO:

> He's the best visionary I've ever met and a huge leader in our space. I love talking to our colleagues and clients about times when he was thinking years ahead of the curve and I've been able to see it come to reality. Similarly, I've heard him introduce me and refer to my being an expert in our space and in our business, seeing and managing operations like it was a fun creative space (which, to me, it is). We all have flaws and limitations, but highlighting those to anybody doesn't have a net positive impact. Instead, focus on strengths and build relationships.

ERIK CHURCH AND ROY DISNEY

While I'm talking about making each other look good, I want to share some thoughts from a close friend and Acacia fraternity brother I've known since 1987 who now does my old job at 1-800-GOT-JUNK?: Erik Church. I asked Erik for his thoughts on how a CEO and COO work together. What he sent me was so powerful I asked him if I could put it in the book:

EVERY MAGICIAN'S INVISIBLE HAND

Disney.

Just two syllables is all it takes to conjure the memory of a man who's made hundreds of millions of people smile. The world has admired the magical mind of Walt Disney for nearly a hundred years.

I admire his older brother, Roy.

Walt was clearly the visionary behind the magic, but his brother Roy helped bring Walt's visions into reality.

Even though Roy Disney was a co-founder, it was not "Disney Brothers" or "Disney Enterprises." It was "The Walt Disney Company." There can be only one CEO, one iconic visionary, one lightning rod to pull power from the sky.

We know it takes every player in the band to make the music come alive, but the public needs a figure to focus on. This is why nearly every famous band has an obvious lead singer.

I am fortunate to partner with Brian Scudamore, the visionary of our business, O2E Brands.

Like Roy Disney, I too am a co-founder, but I never refer to myself that way. I feel strongly that every iconic leader should be elevated and supported by their COO, never feeling they are in competition with them.

Brian and I are famously unified in our vision and in the direction of our path forward, but it doesn't always begin that way. In private, we arm wrestle. In public, we are aligned.

A COO should be the implementer of the CEO's vision. This requires the COO to have the ego strength to judge himself or herself only by the achievement of outstanding results, without any need for public credit or affirmation. There can only be one Winston Churchill, one Steve Jobs, and one Elon Musk— even though each of these men was supported by people who implemented their vision and brought their music to life.

When I have worked for weaker CEOs, I have had to step into the CEO role. Although I did a reasonably good job, I found it to be exhausting. To do the job of CEO, I had to contort myself out of my natural shape to such a degree that I finally concluded it wasn't sustainable or healthy.

When Brian approached me to be his COO, we created a list of our strengths and weaknesses and found that we were a perfect fit. He is strong where I am weak, and I am strong where he is weak. We are two sides of one coin. This serves our company, as we approach every challenge from a different perspective. Then, after much deliberation, we land on an informed path decided by Brian, our CEO.

Our ego is loosely defined as our conscious mind, that part of our identity that we consider our "self." By this definition, the COO must be "selfless" during working hours, wearing only the cloak of the company, subservient to its vision and its culture as set by the CEO.

The COO must be comfortable with his or her ego strength and forego the need for control.

Otherwise, anything with two heads is a monster.

Erik Church, COO,

O2E Brands: 1-800-GOT-JUNK?, WOW 1 DAY PAINTING, Shack Shine

ERIK'S BELIEFS

- The best CEO succession plan is rarely the COO.
- The COO should never be in competition with the CEO.
- The CEO is the external embodiment of the company; the COO is the internal coach of the company.
- The CEO is the lifeblood of the organization, and the COO is the heart that keeps blood coursing through the organization's body.
- Great COOs are rarely great CEOs...and vice versa.

DATE NIGHT

"Date night" is a time for you and your COO to get away from the office and day-to-day demands of work. Make time just to hang out and build a relationship as humans who happen to run a company together. You might play squash or golf, go for a run, visit a bar, or grab coffee.

I recommend setting a regular time, preferably weekly, to develop the foundation of trust and friendship that will benefit everyone you supervise and serve. Deepening the CEO-COO relationship has the capacity to supercharge the organization.

Date night can take many different forms, but the key is to get away from the office—whether it's going to someone's home or to a club or a retreat. Brian and I used to work from the tennis club. Sometimes, we'd be on our computers next to each other and wouldn't talk for two and a half hours; at other times, we'd chat about six different things. Time away from the office builds trust and offers a better opportunity to communicate without interruptions. A regular change of environment makes for a better, more collaborative relationship.

TJ Hock, COO and Partner at Rentwell Maintenance Services, says of his relationship with his CEO: "We take trips twice a year to connect. One of them is usually themed around spirituality as well as business. We also read the same books and talk about them. Our families get together occasionally." He says all these points of contact have "built trust between" the two of them and led to "an incredible bond" for which he is "so very thankful."

In surveying seconds in command for this book, I heard from

one COO who noted, "We spend a lot of time together and brainstorm on all key topics. The bedrock [of our trust] is the personal relationship that we have built over time."

SKIP-LEVEL MEETINGS

Skip-level meetings can be delicate, because they involve the CEO talking to the COO's reports without the COO. The purpose isn't to undermine the COO, but rather to maintain relationships and generate ideas to discuss with the COO later. Done well, these meetings can have a positive effect on organizational advancement—but done badly, they can cause disruption and confusion.

If you've agreed that marketing now reports to the COO, for example, after a few months you will lose touch with what marketing is doing because you're no longer in all the meetings or dealing with the team. Periodically, it might be useful for you to skip over the top of the COO and marketing head to sit down with the marketing team and ask questions, walk through the numbers, and receive a briefing on what the department is doing and how it's going.

A CEO skips the COO and meets with reports for one of two reasons: to get feedback about a potential initiative or to get feedback about what could improve in the organization. Potential initiatives might include launching a new product or marketing strategy where it would be good for leadership to know what the teams think. Getting feedback to improve is more open-ended: what's going wrong, and what can we do better?

It's no different from a CEO speaking to customers, which

involves skipping over sales, marketing, operations, and customer service. You can take what you learn and bring it back to the business areas involved for more context.

Whatever employees or business area heads answer, it's your job as CEO to say, "That's interesting," "Thank you for your input," or "I like that." It's not your job to commit to taking any particular action in a meeting. In fact, it's important not to commit. If you're used to working without a COO, it's tempting to take the feedback you receive and run with it. That's natural. You hear about a problem, and you want to fix it. That's likely how you've always operated. Now, though, you have a second-in-command who oversees the people you're meeting with, and that partner might have other ideas or more background you're not aware of.

That's why you don't commit without knowing the whole story. The COO will know about politics within the team and who does or doesn't have the skills to address a particular situation. Your job is to learn, observe, and ask questions—but not to make commitments or solve problems. If you commit to a solution without the COO's insight, it could cause a bigger problem. Instead of jumping to action, reflect on what you've heard and ask, "Do you mind if I share that with the COO?" or "Could you share that with the COO?"

When you follow this guidance, skip-level meetings offer a great way to gain insights, generate ideas, and form connections with people who don't report directly to you. In some cases, you may have a good-cop/bad-cop dynamic. Tell the reports you'll take their feedback and sit with it. They don't need an immediate fix; they just appreciate being heard.

Waiting and conferring is essential for such meetings to work, because otherwise you get a situation similar to when a child plays one parent against the other. As COO Alliance member and LineDrive EVP Anthony R. Crissie says, making unilateral decisions "creates distrust and usually results in missed steps in the process." Maybe the COO already said no to a particular idea, and you don't want to undermine their authority. Employees aren't necessarily trying to be manipulative, but a lack of coordination between CEO and COO will have a negative impact.

Part of the CEO's job is to always shine a spotlight on the COO. If the CEO makes unilateral operational decisions, the COO gets unintentionally undermined. Your job is to gain information that can help the COO do *their* job. You help the COO see what's coming that they might not otherwise see, but you don't do their job for them.

As the CEO, it's not your responsibility to get involved in business areas that you've delegated to the COO. However, it's good to have leadership team meetings to ensure everyone stays on the same page and that the organization continues moving toward your Vivid Vision. The COO, in turn, needs to constantly stay up to speed on the CEO's vision for the company. If you stay on the same page, there's no need to play catch-up.

If you're having a contractor build you a home, you will likely visit the site periodically to see how it's going and ask clarifying questions, but you'll let the contractor get on with the building. The contractor, meanwhile, will likely need to check in with you periodically to make sure they're interpreting your vision correctly and see if it needs tweaking—but they don't tell you what kind of house you should want to live in. You need to stay in your respective roles while also staying on the same page.

In considering best practices for skip-levels, Griff Long of OrangeTheory Fitness says, "There is a delicate balance to be considered when the COO's direct reports may have a closer or longer relationship with the CEO. While being onboarded as the COO, it is important for one to develop a strong relationship with their direct reports so that there is a consistent narrative being carried through when the CEO performs a skip level."

DELEGATE, DELEGATE, DELEGATE

Knowing what I know now, I would have delegated even more, even faster at 1-800-GOT-JUNK?. Earlier on, I would have put a greater focus on growing and aligning people—and doing less myself. Because I came in as the mentor and had previously done similar work, I tended to do tasks myself when I could have focused more on employee growth. I probably could have scaled the organization even better and faster had I gotten out of my own way.

If you're moving quickly, whether as a CEO or COO, you need to intentionally pause to ask yourself who else could do what you're doing and how you could grow people. When I started, my main question was, "How quickly can I get this done?" I didn't feel threatened, because there was no worry about being put out of a job; every time I hired more smart people, there was more to do. However, I learned it was important to balance short-term speed with long-term efficiency.

I could have multiplied my results by getting good people to do more of the work earlier, rather than doing it myself. At the pace that we were growing, I should have been spending more of my time recruiting, growing, and aligning people. Early on, Brian didn't direct me on shifting this focus; but after about a year, he pushed me in the direction of getting out of the day-to-day.

When we were first building, I used to send our franchisees weekly metrics on how they were doing compared to each other on the measurable parts of their business. Whenever I would send out the dashboard, there was always a minor mistake or a less-than-optimal presentation. One day, one of my team members asked to send it out for me. Their version was way better than mine, and by delegating the task—or being forced to delegate it—I freed up all those hours. It's about getting shit done, not about doing it yourself.

As a CEO, it's important to notice if your COO is trying to do everything themselves, because in that scenario, they're not scaling. A scalable approach is bringing people in and continuing to grow them.

DON'T BURN OUT

Sunil Rajasekar, President and CTO at Mindbody, says he would advise his twenty-two-year-old self, "Don't burn out. You're not invincible."

COOs risk burnout when they don't keep themselves in balance. Sometimes they forget that the job is not a sprint. If they work fifty- to seventy-hour weeks and skip vacations, they'll show up stressed and unbalanced and fail to give the best advice. Burnout leads to missed opportunities.

Of course, a CEO is in danger of burnout, too. That's why you need a COO who helps resist the madness rather than getting sucked into it.

At one point as a COO, I surveyed my direct reports and asked what area of the business I could get better at. Many said I needed to take more time off, be more relaxed, and show up less stressed. If I did, they said, they would be more inspired. They didn't want to feel like the only way they could succeed in their job was by being a workaholic.

A COO's work is never done. They'll never get it all done or get fully caught up. There's always more to do toward building the business, but they need to stay in harmony and think strategically rather than succumbing to the temptation of solving everyone's problems for them. It's a question of mastering work-life balance.

The COO needs to remember that their job is to grow people so that they can solve their own problems and make their own decisions. Getting sucked into doing the work instead of growing people to do the work means a COO will never have a life.

As a CEO, if you see your COO working around the clock, it's a sign of a big problem. Culturally, something isn't working in the organization. An overworked COO will not inspire their team. Instead of putting in eighty hours a week, they need to systematize and automate so that the business can scale. As Michael Gerber puts it, they need to work more *on* the business than *in* it. It's particularly toxic when both the CEO and COO are workaholics.

If working is your hobby, you're creating a dangerous culture in the organization—because most of the people who work for you aren't there as a hobby; they're there because it's their job.

ONGOING COMMUNICATION

In addition to nonwork bonding, the CEO and COO should also carve out time for regular connection on business issues. Years ago, when I was reporting to the CEO of Boyd Autobody, I said that I wanted to have a weekly one-hour call with him. He said he didn't need a weekly call, and I replied, "Maybe not, but I do." I needed the time to bounce ideas, talk about what I was working on to make sure we were aligned, ask for coaching or support, and check in on the rest of the business in order to execute my job most effectively.

The CEO and COO need to engage in ongoing communication to make sure they're up to date on what each is working on and struggling with. Keeping lines of communication open also allows you to adjust and redefine roles if needed. You may need to reshuffle six, twelve, or eighteen months in, which will require a discussion, but you'll have a much better sense of what needs to happen and what the next steps should be if you've stayed on the same page.

The formal structure of a weekly same-page meeting works best to keep the collaboration in balance. With Brian, we had a weekly one-on-one for an hour and then a weekly offsite to reinforce our connection. We also frequently got together for lunch, drinks, coffee, or a run. We continually communicated and had stretches of working side by side to stay in sync.

We also had a weekly leadership team meeting to stay on the same page and a monthly leadership meeting specifically regarding financials and twelve-month strategic planning and brainstorming. Quarterly, we'd meet about the quarterly plan, and then annually, we'd meet for two days to work on the annual financial plan. Everyone needs to be in the loop regarding the plan as far ahead as you've strategized.

CHAPTER 9

WHAT DO I DO NOW?

"We have a strong work culture where the spotlight gets shined on lots of different people, beyond the CEO and myself. Overall, we both have a strong sense of self-worth."

—ROB DAVIES, PRESIDENT, JAM GROUP

A COO changes the dynamics and the way the organization accomplishes work—but the scale of that change can come as a surprise. You hired a second-in-command to help get responsibilities off your plate so you can focus on your Unique Abilities, but old habits can die hard, and it's not always easy for a CEO to let go. When your role changes, it's natural to feel unsure about how to react, so make sure you're reflecting on the best uses of your time and energy so you can avoid becoming a source of resistance to the COO.

It bears repeating that you must know yourself well before you ever bring in a second-in- command. If you can't work with a competent COO or you feel threatened by letting them do their job, then you've hit a leadership ceiling and will hamstring yourself. As a CEO, you need to learn vulnerability. This person is there as your partner—not a threat. It's still *your* business. And you can fire them if you need to.

There's no reason to feel intimidated. You're paying someone to do a job for you, so let them get on with it.

LEARNING TO LET GO

That doesn't make the transition easy, necessarily. As CEO, you're going from having the whole company depend on you to having a COO who does much of the heavy lifting. What should you do with all the time you gain?

Rather than grasping at responsibility or authority, effective leadership requires learning to let go. Your job is to get results *through* people. You ensure the business scales and all the work gets done—but not by you.

As you begin letting go of some of what you used to do, you'll have time to spend on what gives you energy and what you're best at. You can plan for the future, observe, hold skip-levels, do deep dives into different business areas, and report back with what you find.

Your job is to think strategically rather than be down in the trenches. While a COO gets on with execution and heavy lifting, you can slow down enough to converse, listen, and give timely feedback where it's needed. It might feel like you're not getting anything done, but this thoughtful leadership is hugely important.

Once you free up your time and energy, you can make better decisions with major implications. One of my coaching clients, for instance, sat down with his team and asked them to make a list of all the projects they were working on. He discovered they had almost 200 projects underway across the company. It was a ridiculous number, because they only really had time to work on ten or twelve—so he completely eliminated 150. When he showed me the list of what he had eliminated, I made him throw it out. He'd wanted to keep those 150 ideas for later, but I knew he would never need them. They had plenty of ideas.

Because he was able to slow down and think, he probably de-stressed the organization by 10X. They no longer needed to worry about random responsibilities of little value. Now they could focus on the critical few.

If you find it difficult to let go, try looking at what you're gaining rather than what you're losing. Having someone else take work off your plate is a privilege rather than a hardship. You've earned the chance to free up more time to focus on strategy and your biggest strengths and passions in the business.

If you've hired someone to manage five business areas that used to report to you, it's important to figure out what your new job is. How do you spend time thinking about strategy? How do you spend time working with the board? How do you spend time to better understand the industry? How do you observe the organization from a distance, and which areas are you best at where you could spend more time? Figuring out your new responsibilities and how to deal with them will allow the COO to work on their own responsibilities.

DON'T SCATTER SHIT

Working with a COO is to a large extent about not getting in each other's way. Remember that you're hiring an expert to come in and run the business for you or to run a number of areas of the business. You need to let them do that. If you bring them in to run the business, let them run it, which means getting out of the way. Of course, to do so, you need to trust them. Yes, ask questions, but don't micromanage or engage in "seagull management"—that's what I call a scenario in which the CEO swoops in, shits all over everything, and leaves.

Entrepreneurs tend to feel like they're adding value or identifying something that frustrates them, so they intervene, but then they realize they're too busy or don't want to deal with it, so they fly off. It's much better to pull the COO aside and share what you saw or what frustrated you privately. Then, let them go take care of the fix. Follow the same principles as the skip-level meetings by reporting back and conferring rather than by taking over. On a recent call with Jason Hennessey (CEO of Hennessey Digital) and his COO Scott Shrum, who is also a COO Alliance member, Jason said, "Things are going too well right now. I'm not sure what to focus on. I feel like I need to break some stuff to get engaged again."

Entrepreneurial founder CEOs are also often starved for praise, which makes sense. As I've said so many times on stages, I feel like we're all just sixteen-year-olds trapped in adult bodies. We're all still dealing with our teenage insecurities in some way. If someone else comes into your company and starts sharing the praise, accolades, and recognition with your teams, it's natural to feel less loved or less secure. Recognize, though, that people think more of you because of who you've brought in help to grow the company.

It's dangerous to interfere, thinking you can fix a problem faster than the COO because there will be repercussions. You start to undermine them when your job is actually to shine the spotlight on them. If you swoop in to do something, you're actually hurting that COO's ability to do more inside the company, even if that's not your intention. The job of the CEO is to grow the skills and the confidence of the COO.

DELEGATION AND UNIQUE ABILITY TEAMS

Dan Sullivan, who built Strategic Coach, talks about building Unique Ability teams based on the areas of strength that you're most passionate about and energized by. Delegate everything except genius. Get everything off your plate except your Unique Abilities. If you're great at speaking and dealing with the media, do those 80 percent of the time. Do more speaking, more talking to the media, and more outreach, and then spend the rest of your time thinking and observing the industry, not doing the COO's job.

Most CEOs still keep three to five business areas reporting to them, or whatever is a manageable number. You might keep finance or marketing because you love that area. Maybe you keep legal and compliance for strategic reasons. I'm sure Steve Jobs kept product reporting to him, but I doubt that he had the retail experience reporting to him. He often talked about product design and marketing, but he didn't have a whole lot to say about retail.

The key is to identify the areas of the business you're best at leading and that give you energy—the ones that harness your Unique Abilities. Delegate everything else. If you make the right COO hire, someone who loves and excels at what you don't, then everything gets done and people gain energy and fulfillment in the process. On the other hand, if you hire a COO who wants to oversee areas in your Unique Abilities, there is bound to be friction.

Delegation represents a way to supercharge the growth of the organization. You have more time to work on what gives you energy, which allows you to bring that energy into the rest of the business instead of transferring stress and a sense of being overwhelmed throughout the company.

Have the COO build the teams such that each person only works on *their* Unique Ability areas. To build Unique Ability teams, the COO should start with having every key leader do the activity inventory, making a spreadsheet of every task they do over the course of a normal month. Column A lists the tasks. In column B, rank them by Incompetent, Competent, Excellent, and Unique Ability. The first step is getting everything off their plates that they're incompetent or only competent at. Next is to redistribute some of the excellent tasks to other executives so that they're left only working on their Unique Abilities.

It often isn't your job as CEO to engage in strategies like building UA teams, but it's a tremendous point of leverage when a COO does.

CONFLICT AT THE TOP

Despite the care you took in hiring the right COO, you're not always going to get along. The key with conflict is to remember that, as in a marriage, it's natural. When you're spending so much time passionately engaged in an endeavor with another person, there will sometimes be differences, miscommunication, mismatched energy, and stress. Both people are trying their best, but sometimes life intervenes.

When addressing conflict, focus on what went wrong, what you need in the future, and how you feel about what happened. Ask the other person how they're feeling, as well. Remember that you're upset with a result, not with the person. You don't like an output, but the person is not the problem.

Work through the situation, get your feelings out in a compassionate way, and make sure the other person knows you still care about them. You value the relationship, but this specific issue isn't working for you. State specifically what has frustrated you, and let them air their side, too.

COO Alliance member and Redirect Health COO Guy Berry emphasizes the importance of not making conflict personal: "The big thing is, words are words. They can't hurt you... If you let those words hurt you and break you down mentally as a leader, you're just not going to be able to last. It's going to tear you apart."

Address the specific issue. If you're upset because the COO shows up late, explain what you felt in that specific situation and why, rather than snapping, "You're always late to meetings." Remember, you're stronger together than you are apart, and working through the rough patches leads to strength. You're always busy, growing, and working hard, so it's better to work with the person through trust than to demolish everything the second it gets hard.

Deal with conflict in private, because arguing in front of employees or the board will send negative ripples throughout the organization. Find a way to engage in healthy disagreement without burdening the leadership team or board of advisors. If you constantly argue and debate things in front of others, you undermine the whole foundation of the organization.

You need to figure out how to work together, even when you have different perspectives. Don't go to HR to solve a conflict. HR can coach you on how to go back and solve the conflict for yourself, but they should not serve as the arbiter. HR's job is to teach people how to solve their own issues, not to become the union steward or do the uncomfortable relational work for people.

Managing conflict is much easier when you've built a solid foundation through date nights and shared activities that transcend work and cultivate personal connection. If you've grown trust and mutual respect, then a conflict won't destroy the relationship.

Remember that the COO benefits *you*, whether by shortening your work week, growing the company, or expanding your capacity and capabilities. Stay focused on those benefits. You can work through difficult times in service of the positives. When you air conflict, though, it's like parents fighting in front of their kids and unnecessarily scaring them for days. It creates a negative butterfly effect throughout the organization instead of resolving your conflict together with each other.

At the end of the day, it's your company. You're ultimately responsible. Even if you're not the owner or founder, the buck still stops with you. However, that doesn't mean you can run the business as "my way or the highway," because you'll hurt the culture of the organization and undermine the whole point of bringing in a COO. Being too controlling or too much of a hard-ass will lead to churn. You need to flip the org chart upside down and focus on your role as the chief energizing officer who supports the leadership team that supports the managers who support the employees. Manage conflict and foster relationships for the good of the organization.

AVOIDING EGO

The COO needs to come in with humility and drive, building consensus and building teams. They can't come in as an auto-cratic dictatorial leader, because they won't earn respect. As I've said, the employees in the company will respect the COO title, but they also need to respect the person who's in that seat. Ego undermines that goal.

CEOs, too, should be wary of ego. You should have confidence, but ego is dangerous. It leads to back channeling, lack of motivation, and employee turnover. People don't want to work for assholes. They want to work for confident people, but you need to check your ego at the door. As Jim Collins talked about in *Good to Great*, Level 5 leadership includes a "blend of personal humility and personal will."

Ego can seem charismatic at first, but then it turns people off and undermines success. You don't need to be self-effacing, but you do need humility.

COOs have to check their ego at the door and be okay with the fact that the CEO will get most of the limelight. The CEO tends to garner the fame and accolades, and a good COO will have the temperament not to care.

In some cases, you might share the limelight. When I worked with Brian at 1-800-GOT-JUNK?, we often shared the limelight because I asked for credit for my part in building the franchise program, a strategic decision to build my personal brand and career. I didn't want to invest six years in making his company what it was and have no way to leverage those accomplishments. At the same time, because I wasn't ego-driven, I was happy to shine the spotlight on him as founder and CEO.

The COO's job is to grow people and instill confidence in each member of the leadership team, allowing them to receive accolades for work well done. The COO doesn't just shine the light up to the founder but also down to other leaders. Doing so requires not needing to swoop in and talk all the credit. Instead, the COO can highlight how great their VPs and directors are. The goal is to grow the skill set of others, not to hoard recognition for themselves.

MAKING AN IMPACT

I saw so many CEOs and entrepreneurs struggling—it felt like watching flies banging their heads on windows trying to get out—and I wanted to help them. It was such a huge need that we had to build the COO Alliance. That has expanded now to hosting the *Second in Command* podcast, helping my clients, and coaching their COOs. I'm also excited about the thousands of managers learning from the content in my Invest in Your Leaders course. Larger companies are increasingly working with us and listening to the *Second in Command* podcast, too. CEOs can gain some good insights from the podcast and see issues from a different perspective. Business interviews tend to focus on the CEO side, so there's an opportunity to expand your perspective to the COO side and use a different lens. We keep gaining traction, scaling, and gaining podcast listeners.

I've made my mark, I feel good about it, and I don't need to be a COO again. Sooner or later, I'll probably have an operations person to whom I can delegate, but I don't think I'll ever need a full COO. I can keep my current projects within my span of control.

Most of the guests on the *Second in Command* podcast are unknown names. I usually find a company, brand, or CEO and want the rest of the story, so I ask for an introduction to their second-in-command. I wanted the story of Rippling, Shopify, and Bumble because they were doing so well that they must have great COOs, but I didn't know their names when I started.

My podcast is often the first place people really get to know COOs. Many aren't used to interfacing with the media, whereas CEOs tend to do so frequently. I love the chance to get the unvarnished rest of the story about business growth that we don't typically hear when we only talk to entrepreneurs. It's like only hearing moms' opinions on child-rearing, when of course dads have their own valid perspective, too.

One of the only COOs whose name most people know is Sheryl Sandberg; she was with Facebook for 15 years as COO before announcing that she was stepping down. Before joining Facebook, Sandberg was vice president of global online sales and operations at Google. Before that, she was the chief of staff for the United States secretary of the treasury. The COO is akin to a politician's chief of staff, and that label has become popular in the business world.

Mark Zuckerberg has shone the light on her to make sure she's world-famous for having been his second-in-command. As a result, she was okay with remaining COO because she got the accolades and people knew she built the company alongside Zuckerberg—in addition to receiving generous financial compensation, of course. Zuckerberg has openly admitted that in the early days she was there as his babysitter and helper, although she later became his partner.

Most COOs are not trying to move into the CEO role or grow their careers beyond the COO level. They are happy and well suited to growing the organization until their skill set no longer serves. Their satisfaction comes from their contribution and from fair compensation, not necessarily from any wider recognition. Often, COOs appreciate autonomy and increasing opportunities, such as extra PTO to work on an executive MBA. COO satisfaction comes from feeling like they're doing great work, working with great people, and being paid fairly for their time.

The personality type is such that most don't want the limelight, or the stress of the CEO role. When I asked one COO for their reflections to include in this book, they thanked me for the opportunity but said, "I respectfully decline, as I prefer to be in the background and not the spotlight." They said they take their cues from Roy Disney, who made his brother Walt's magic run on time from behind the scenes. They quoted Roy Disney as saying, "It's not hard to make decisions when you know what your values are."

CHAPTER 10

THE PARTY'S OVER

"It's all going to be okay. I didn't grow up with much, and the anxiety and the fear of where my next meal was going to come from have always fueled me. Every job I've been in, I've always thought, 'I'm going to be fired at any moment, so I have to do the best possible job.' There's a lot of good that comes out of that. There are also a lot of wasted cycles."

—TOM KEISER, COO AT ZENDESK

As much as you invest energy into finding a COO, and as much as you build a true friendship with your second-in-command, the CEO-COO team is rarely for life. Smaller companies starting out have different needs from large, established ones trying to level up. All businesses go through different phases, and it's unlikely that a single COO will be suitable for all of them—even though the CEO remains in place.

As circumstances and businesses change, a time may come for the current COO to move on. This chapter talks about when you know it's time, how to go about the process—and what to look for next.

THE CONSEQUENCES OF CHANGE

To stay in the same job, a COO's skill set has to continue matching the organization as it scales, which is often a challenge. By contrast, the CEO can usually stick to their same skill set, as long as they're good at hiring the right people to take work off their plate. As a CEO, you need to continually grow your interpersonal, delegation, and soft skills of leadership—but not the actual tactical skills of running different business areas. One job isn't easier than the other; they're just different.

The COO role changes as a business matures, and the projects the COO is responsible for change as a result. If that person can't continue to scale and keep their skills in alignment, at some point they'll be out of a job.

The COO fit is similar to sports. You might be the best hockey player on the team when you're twelve, but when you're twenty, the demands are different. You won't be the best unless your skills have kept up.

How do you know when it's time for the COO to leave? It's when they can't get the results needed, when the company is substantially different from what it was when they joined, or they're no longer enjoying it. As in a marriage, the COO and CEO both grow, but sometimes they grow apart and are no longer compatible. Sometimes the COO falls out of love with the job, or the CEO and COO no longer work well together.

You'll sense it. As soon as you have doubt, then you have no doubt. When the relationship no longer feels right, it's not right. If you know as a CEO that the COO can no longer get the results you need, cannot bring on the necessary teams, or can no longer stay above the fray as the company scales, it's time to think about a successor.

Most senior people can only take a business through two doubles in revenue. The third double makes it hard for them to continue doing the job. A COO could enter a $10 million company that goes to $20 million and then $40 million, but it's unlikely they'll do well running it as an $80 million company. A COO who begins with a fifty-person company that goes to one hundred and then two hundred will likely struggle to deliver when it hits four hundred people. Unless they've intentionally grown and adapted their skills, they're likely out of a job.

As the COO's fit declines, they'll get more and more frazzled and have less and less fun. COOs might have the self-awareness to see when their tenure is ending, but you can't rely on that. A CEO *has* to know for themselves.

GETTING FIRED

When Brian brought me in to help him build 1-800-GOT-JUNK?, it had $2 million in annual revenue, and only twelve franchises. Then it went to $6 million, then $16 million, then $34 million. By the time it reached $106 million, it felt huge to me. The company had gone from fourteen people at the head office to 248, and from twelve locations to 330. We had three thousand employees system-wide.

Brian now needed a highly detail-oriented COO, but that isn't my skill set. Whereas I had been an excellent fit when we were scaling, the role had changed, and my contribution had fallen off. My strength is entrepreneurial growth and using my intuition. If a CEO wants rapid growth and franchising, I'm their person. Once that phase is over, they don't need me anymore. They need a different Cameron.

The Wednesday night Brian asked to meet for breakfast at the Vancouver club in the morning, I told his assistant that he was going to fire me. She said, "Oh, shut up—go home and spend time with your kids," but my intuition told me it was over. The next morning at 7:30 a.m., Brian said, "I think we're done." I started to cry, and so did he. I said, "I think you're right."

In fact, I knew he was right. I wasn't enjoying it as much anymore. I was frustrated with aspects of the company that the leadership team didn't seem to see. They wanted a plan and budget which called for adding way more franchises than I knew were available, as our areas were largely getting sold out. I thought we had to grow our individual franchises bigger, but I didn't have the skills to explain the situation to get people to see what I saw. I was finally out of my league.

I was at a stage of my career where I wanted to figure out what I would be best at doing next. I was forty-two years old, had helped build this highly successful company, had helped build a couple of others before that, and I didn't want to be operational anymore. I wanted to have control of my time and life to do what I wanted to do when I wanted to do it.

I took three and a half months off to journal and figure out my plan forward. I got more than thirty job offers during that time, but I was done with that chapter of my life. I decided to reinvent myself and look at all the things that I was best at and how to leverage them. I started coaching CEOs, doing speaking events, and solely focusing on my Unique Abilities.

After roughly twelve months of searching for my replacement, Brian brought in the former president of Starbucks to replace me as COO. The company had grown to a size where I felt in over my head, but to her, it was small and cute. We were looking at the same business from an entirely different perspective.

She was more corporate and used to working on larger company initiatives. She understood cross-functional and matrix decision-making. Brian felt he could delegate and let her run the business for him. I thought it was a brilliant hire, but it turned out to be disastrous because she wasn't the right cultural fit. She was fired a year later, even though she had the skill set to do the job.

Next, Brian brought in Erik Church, who has both the cultural fit and the skill set and has now been COO for almost ten years. He was exactly the right person to take the company from $100 million to $1 billion. I've known him since we started a fraternity together in Ottawa, Canada, in 1987. I was president the first year, and he was president the second year. We also both worked at College Pro Painters. I was COO at 1-800-GOT-JUNK? first, followed by him.

Erik is absolutely the right person to take the business to the next level, but he would have been terrible as the first COO because that earlier era needed someone like me who really knew how to grow a franchise company almost from scratch. I would have been terrible at growing it when he did. I knew how to scale the franchising, and he knows how to run a larger organization. Erik says the role of the COO is "providing a vision...for what the growth of the individual means." He's been one of the all-time best hires Brian has ever made.

Brian made a great choice in two of three cases—which shows that hiring the right COO is difficult but—when done right—really worthwhile.

STAY ALIGNED OR MOVE ON

If the COO stops buying into your Vivid Vision, they should leave. The essence of their purpose is to make your dreams for the business a reality. If they don't like those dreams, they should go find other dreams to implement. If they hadn't been aligned during the interview process, you wouldn't have hired them. So, if you grow apart later—maybe your Vivid Vision changes after several years of working together—you have to be just as clear-sighted. If they're not onboard, they're out (and if their skills no longer match the new vision, they're also out).

The COO is like a booster rocket. They push you higher and higher. And when they burn out at a certain level, which they usually do, you can hire a new one to take you to the next level. That's what's perfect about finding the right COO. Even when you feel like your business has gone as far as it can go, there's a COO out there who can take you further.

This book has shown you how to find them. Now all you have to do is start looking!

PART 4

APPENDIX

SECOND IN COMMAND PODCAST: THE TOP TWENTY-ISH

The *Second in Command* podcast is where I interview the chief operating officer behind the chief executive officer to learn their tips, systems, and insights from being the second-in-command of an amazing growth company. I gain incredible advice by bringing on serious guests who have accomplished some serious things. It's a must-listen if you are trying to run your organization efficiently and grow it properly. The *Second in Command* podcast is brought to you by the COO Alliance, where top-level COOs share the insights, tactics, and strategies that have made them the Chief Behind the Chief.

Everyone else interviews CEOs. I want the rest of the story.

Check out some of the most outstanding and insightful episodes from the series. Better still, listen to all 200-plus episodes on cooalliance.com/podcasts.

EPISODE	COMPANY	NAME	TITLE	LINK
2	1-800-GOT-JUNK?	Erik Church	COO	https://cooalliance.com/podcasts-1800gotjunk
3	Shopify	Harley Finkelstein	COO	https://cooalliance.com/podcasts-shopify
40	YPO	Sean Magennis	President and COO	https://cooalliance.com/podcasts-ypo
43	Cleveland Indians	Brian Barrens	COO	https://cooalliance.com/podcasts-cleveland-indians
45	Bumble	Sarah Jones Simmer	COO	https://cooalliance.com/podcasts-bumble
48	ZenDesk	Tom Keiser	COO	https://cooalliance.com/podcasts-zendesk
49	BulletProof Coffee	Anna Collins	President and COO	https://cooalliance.com/podcasts-bulletproof
51	Khan Academy	Ginny Lee	COO	https://cooalliance.com/podcasts-khan-academy
59	Mind Valley	Kshitij Minglani	Co-Founder	https://cooalliance.com/podcasts-mindvalley
82	Hello Sign	Whitney Bouck	COO	https://cooalliance.com/podcasts-hellosign
83	15Five	Shane Metcalf	Co-Founder and COO	https://cooalliance.com/podcasts-15five
85	ClickFunnels	Ryan Montgomery	COO	https://cooalliance.com/podcasts-clickfunnels
90	Poshmark	John McDonald	COO	https://cooalliance.com/podcasts-poshmark
92	Orange Theory	Griff Long	COO	https://cooalliance.com/podcasts-orange-theory
114	Rippling	Matt MacInnis	COO	https://cooalliance.com/podcasts-rippling
130	Wikimedia	Janeen Uzzell	COO	https://cooalliance.com/podcasts-wikimedia
139	Hint Water	Theo Goldin	COO	https://cooalliance.com/podcasts-hint
172	LifeAid	Andy Halliday	COO	https://cooalliance.com/podcasts-lifeaid
178	Clubhouse	Maya Watson	Head of Global Marketing	https://cooalliance.com/podcasts-clubhouse
182	Blockchain.com	Lane Kasselman	Chief Business Officer	https://cooalliance.com/podcasts-blockchain
194	Mindbody	Sunil Rajasekar	President and CTO	https://cooalliance.com/podcasts-mindbody
198	Asana	Anne Raimondi	COO and Head of Business	https://cooalliance.com/podcasts-asana
200	Mighty Capital	Jennifer Vancini	General and Founding Partner	https://cooalliance.com/podcasts-mighty-capital

COO ALLIANCE

The COO Alliance is designed to support the second-in-command, improving upon their skills and equipping them with the tools necessary to further grow within their roles, and to grow their company in the process.

Each and every member is vetted to ensure they're an exceptional community fit, so networking dynamics run smoothly and effectively.

This is the only membership in the world that is offered exclusively to COOs, GMs and VPs.

MEMBERSHIP BENEFITS

If your organization is currently generating more than $5M in annual revenue, you're invited to have your COO apply for COO Alliance membership, which includes:

- twelve monthly three-hour online events with members from seventeen countries
- networking opportunities so they can learn from a vetted group of other COO professionals
- ability to attend workshops and training via Zoom from anywhere in the world
- exclusive guest speakers for every event of the year
- presentations from peers ready to share their own insights and knowledge
- confidential access to member contact info
- exclusive private Slack workgroup and channels
- access to past event speakers and peer videos so they can learn with the group even when they're not able to attend in person
- private Slack group to share resources and ask for help

10X GUARANTEE...

Your COO can come to any In-Person event or join our online program for the year. Both are backed by our 10X Guarantee:

> After actively participating during your annual membership, if you don't get at least ten times the value of your investment back in the form of savings and projected profits from attending, we'll give you your money back. No questions asked.

However, no one has ever needed to take us up on that promise.

With the 10X guarantee, it's irresponsible to not have your COO at least attend one in-person event or try out a first year with us online.

As a CEO, it's your responsibility to ensure the company continues to grow, and that means reinvesting in your team.

Don't miss out on this highly valuable opportunity to boost your revenue, streamline your operations, and have your COO network with other C-level executives.

SAMPLE COO SCORECARD

The scorecard is based on the book *Topgrading*, known as the top book for interviewing, recruiting, and hiring senior people. The book talks about the scorecard as a measurable way to know if someone is the right fit to hire. It's two or three pages long.

This example is from a real client I coached. We created it when he was getting ready to interview for a COO position.

COO Scorecard

The Mission of the COO is to grow revenues by executing on XXX's vision and mentor existing employees.

	Outcomes	COMMENTS AND RATING
1	**Profitably grow revenues 100% a year for the next 4 years** a. Develop a time table of the company's action plan to achieve at least 100% growth for the next 4 years (2015 - 2018) b. Break the plan into executable steps for the staff, if further staff is required, hire and communicate plan c. Hold staff accountable and responsible for executing their areas d. Turn repeatable projects into systemizable processes e. Identify and eliminate growth bottlenecks within the company to achieve growth targets	Importance: HIGH
2	**Launch 200 new products over the next 30 months** a. Manage product development team to launch products on a defined schedule b. Manage Amazon Manager and website to develop plans for each product's launch to ensure success	Importance: MEDIUM
3	**Launch Vivanaturals.com with $100 million annual recurring revenue** a. Relaunch website with ecommerce, authoritative content and 2 blogs. b. Source award-winning writer for our blog c. Launch YouTube channel with 1 million subscribers d. Launch Webinars e. Build a PR team	Importance: MEDIUM
4	**Build Teams and Mentor Employees** a. Hire and build teams b. Provide leadership coaching to team members on executing, prioritizing, and delivering c. Provide timely feedback to team members to develop/grow d. Set quarterly priorities with each person and coach to achieving targets	Importance: HIGH

The ideal candidate is an Executor in their late 30s/early 40s who has been VP Operations of at least 2 different companies with rapid growth (doubling year over year), is a people's person with a solid work ethic 60+ hours/week, a high performer, relentless executor and does whatever it takes to get the vision executed. We do not need someone with their own ideas, pure execution. We don't need someone with their own strategy, pure execution. The candidate would be the #2 person and the CEOs right hand person. The candidate has scaled companies with rapid growth.

Culture: We're a fun, open concept office. Share lots of laughs and CEO sits outside with everyone. The candidate must be personable and the right balance of friendly/authoritative.

Competencies

COMPETENCIES	COMMENTS AND RATING
Leadership Competencies	
Hires A players	
Develops people	
Removes underperformers	
Treats people with respect	
Efficiency of execution	
Network of talented people	
Flexible/adaptable	
Personal Competencies	
Integrity/honesty	
Organization and planning	
Calm under pressure	
Moves fast	
Time management	
Follows through on commitments	
Intellectual Competencies	
Brainpower/learns quickly	
Analysis skills	
Creative/innovative	
Attention to detail	
Motivational Competencies	
Enthusiasm/ability to motivate others	
Persistent	
Proactivity/takes initiative	
Work ethic	
Sets high standards	
Interpersonal Competencies	
Listening skills	
Open to criticism and others' ideas	
Excellent written communications	
Oral communication	
Teamwork	
Persuasion	
Holds people accountable	
Technical/Functional Competencies	
Asana	
Google Drive	
Knowledge of the industry	
Ecommerce	
Tech Savvy	
Built and managed outsourced/ offshore teams	
Can build software/manage programmers	

A COO MANUAL

Matt MacInnis is a podcast guest who really stands out. He's the COO for a company called Rippling and created what he calls "The Operating Manual to Matt MacInnis." He gives it to all his new employees to understand how to work with him. It explains what makes him tick, what pisses him off, what excites him, what his hot buttons are, and what drives him crazy. By sharing this information, there's no mystery about how he works. I've never seen anything like it—it's brilliant. He has done it with humor and intelligence, and it's a powerful tool.

Here's the full text:

🤓 A LITTLE USER MANUAL FOR MATT MACINNIS

Loosely based on "Working with Claire: An Unauthorized Guide"

ABOUT ME

Grew up in Canada, moved to the US for college. Studied engineering, worked at Apple for seven years, mostly in marketing. I lived in China twice and speak Mandarin pretty well (still study it!). In 2009, I started a company called Inkling, and I sold it in 2018. I joined Rippling in 2019 as COO because of the immense promise of this business. I have a husband and a daughter, both cute.

WHAT I EXPECT OF MYSELF AND OTHERS
Rigorous Thinking and Consistency of Approach

- I appreciate when people know their topic and hew strictly to the facts. I appreciate "I don't know" as an answer. I appreciate when others call (my) bullshit.
- I have a negative reaction to exaggeration, hand-wavy answers, and unsubstantiated assertions or assumptions.
- I appreciate consistency and structured thought ("frameworks," if you will).
- I love working with people who have their own system. I will easily (gleefully!) adapt to your system if I understand it. It is a sign of clear thinking, which is what will help us all succeed together!

Reliability and Grit

I love working with people who...

- ... eat their management broccoli.

- ... proactively deal with the boring, difficult, uncomfortable work.
- ... only need to be told something once.

People like this absorb problems in the organization like activated charcoal; conversely, people who avoid the tough stuff spew problems into the space around them for these people to catch. I try to hold myself to these standards.

The Humility to Learn from Others, *Especially* When It's Inconvenient

I want to debate things, and I hope that we all take well-founded positions in our debates. However, it's hugely important that pride and ego not blind us to new information, no matter how inconvenient. I try hard to keep an open mind about every possibility, and I hope you will too.

The Integrity to Make and Act on the Right Thing to Do, *Especially* When It's Inconvenient

Sometimes, it's really painful to do the right thing, such as proactively notifying customers of an issue they may not otherwise notice, or giving someone difficult feedback when they're already bruised. But I want everyone I work with to always do the right thing—no matter how painful. And I will try to be a force for good in that regard, too.

MY DEMONS
Positive Feedback

I struggle to give positive feedback because it makes me feel a little uncomfortable. I recognize this, and I invite you to call me on it, especially if you don't know where you stand. When I do give feedback, I try hard to make it useful.

Impatient Moods

When I am in get-stuff-done mode, I am sometimes impatient with friendly office banter. I forget to ask how you're doing, and I bristle at attempts to ask me those kinds of questions. Usually, I like to jump into the matters at hand quickly and directly. If I do that, please don't take it personally; it's likely that I care a lot about what you're working on, and I want to get to the meat quickly.

To Be Direct on Hard Things, I Need to Prepare

I think a little more slowly and deeply than some people, which is a blessing and a curse. One side effect is that when I'm forced to think on the spot, I may end up postponing difficult but important conversations. I may brush things aside so that I can buy time to prepare my thoughts.

For conversations that are in my wheelhouse, I am quick to engage and respond. But for tough feedback conversations, for areas I'm not familiar with, or for areas where I lack context, I need to prepare. It is generally ineffective to surprise me with conversation topics, so providing me with context and time to think/process will help me be more effective.

Crassness

I sometimes use crass humor to deflect discomfort, or to build a sense of camaraderie. While humor in the office is generally good, if I say something stupid, please call me on it—or give me googly eyes to let me know I'm being foolish. One management framework calls this the "mischievous derailer," and the name is appropriate.

Overthinking

I can be guilty of overthinking things. I can get caught up in the process or approach instead of staying focused on the quality of output. You can help me by saying, "Matt, you might be overthinking this. I think the answer is probably just X."

HOW TO WORK WITH ME
Communication Channels

- Email is for non-urgent matters. The success rate of reaching me via email is about 90 percent. Assume I will see your email within twenty-four to forty-eight hours, but rarely sooner.
- SMS is for quick or urgent matters. My phone is XXX-XXX-XXXX. I'll generally respond right away. I use WhatsApp regularly, and it's far better than SMS.
- Slack is for conversational matters that aren't urgent. Faster response time, but lower overall success rate of reaching me than via email.

1:1s

- For my direct reports, I default to biweekly, at a consistent time.
- Meetings are structured and purposeful, with a shared 1:1 Google doc.
- Review progress, plans, and problems.
- My goal is to remove obstacles to your success.
- If we don't need the time, we cancel or end early.

Planning

- I like to say what we're going to do.
- I like to do what we said we were going to do.
- I like to change what we said we were going to do as soon as

we realize that it's not the right thing to do (as many times as necessary, until we find what *is* the right thing to do!).

Priorities

I am generally clear-minded and explicit about my priorities. My job is to achieve my priorities. Your job is to achieve your priorities. Our time together, in any context, is best spent at the *intersection* of our respective priorities. I therefore very much appreciate knowing what your priorities are when we talk.

Maker Time vs Manager Time

This is a fast-moving startup, which means I have a lot of stuff that I'm doing directly (i.e., I'm also a maker). If I have my time blocked as "No Meetings," please do not schedule meetings. If you really, really need time with me during those windows, please ask—but the bar will be high. :)

Good Meetings

Please have only the meetings we need, and please ensure those meetings are productive. Always start with an answer to the questions, "What are we trying to accomplish, and how will we know we get there?"

Mutual Development

If we work together, then I want to contribute to your growth. And I invite you to participate in mine. I won't hold back, and I welcome career and development conversations.

KEEP ME HONEST!

What's missing above? Or where am I lying to myself and others? :) All feedback is welcome. The goal is to accelerate our collaboration and improve the effectiveness of our partnership.

FURTHER INFORMATION

AUDIO AND VISUAL

War Room presents: Cameron Herold COOs speaking event
https://www.youtube.com/watch?v=2B51FVd3Za8

I was fired as COO of a $100 Million company (podcast Interview)
https://tinyurl.com/FiredAsCOO

Genius Network Presents: Cameron Herold Vivid Vision speaking event
https://tinyurl.com/GeniusVividVision

TEDx Vancouver: Your Vision Statement Sucks (speaking event)
https://tinyurl.com/TEDxVividVision

CNN Money: Cameron Herold (media interview)
https://tinyurl.com/CameronCNN

WRITTEN WORD

Bennett, Nate, and Stephen A. Miles. "Second in Command: The Misunderstood Role of the Chief Operating Officer." *Harvard Business Review*, May 2006. https://hbr.org/2006/05/second-in-command-the-misunderstood-role-of-the-chief-operating-officer

Bennett, Nate, and Stephen A. Miles. *Riding Shotgun: The Role of the COO*. Stanford Business Books, 2017.

Gil, Elad. *High Growth Handbook: Scaling Startups from 10 to 10,000 People*. Stripe Press, 2018.

Herold, Cameron. *Vivid Vision*. Lioncrest Publishing, 2018.

Wickman, Gino. *Traction: Get a Grip on Your Business*. BenBella Books, 2010.

Wickman, Gino, and Mark C. Winters. *Rocket Fuel: The One Essential Combination that Will Get You More of What You Want from Your Business*. BenBella Books, 2015.

Wikipedia, "COO," accessed September 27, 2022, https://en.wikipedia.org/wiki/Chief_operating_officer

ADVICE FOR COOS FROM COOS

I spoke to many outstanding COOs while I was writing this book. I asked them to reflect on the role of the COO, their relationship with the CEO, and what advice they would give their younger selves. This is insight from the people who know best.

"The COO is that go-to person who is there to keep things moving along, keep the team growing, and see every possible way the organization can be successful, profitable, and healthy overall."

—SCOTT SHRUM, COO, HENNESSEY DIGITAL

"Always have the CEO's best interest in mind. The COO must never sugarcoat the challenges at hand, and the CEO should always expect to always hear firsthand from their COO on the situations being faced."

—GRIFF LONG, COO, ORANGE THEORY FITNESS

"To shine the spotlight on the CEO, the COO should always consider ways in which the CEO can be recognized for being the leader that they are. For instance, in enterprise-wide conferences, the COO could present the CEO prior to their keynote. On the other hand, the CEO also creates opportunities for the COO to be recognized—especially as it relates to meeting or connecting with members of the business operations team."

—GRIFF LONG, COO, ORANGE THEORY FITNESS

"Give the CEO the floor in their strengths and where they get energy, whether it's product or culture, and let their superpower shine"

—ZACH MORRISON, PRESIDENT AND CEO, TINUITI

"We all have flaws and limitations, but highlighting those to anybody doesn't have a net positive impact. Instead, the COO should focus on strengths and build relationships."

—HUNTER MCMAHON, COO, IDISCOVERY SOLUTIONS

"Never stop growing...That would be weird. If it's not technical skills on operations, it's maybe online marketing. If not that, then perhaps it's emotional development, and if not that, maybe it's ingredient sourcing. It's always something."

—RACHEL PACHIVAS, COO, ANNMARIE SKIN CARE

"Believe in people, believe in the power of people, believe in developing people, and believe in providing a vision."

—ERIK CHURCH, COO, O2E BRANDS

"When you're in a company, you're going to have employees who say you are a terrible leader, you're going to have employees who say that you're a bad person. No matter how much you care about those employees, and no matter how much you care

about how they're doing in their lives, there are still going to be people who say stuff. Don't take anything personally."

—GUY BERRY, COO, REDIRECT HEALTH

"No COO on the planet has the same job. Every single one of them has a different job."

—HARLEY FINKELSTEIN, COO, SHOPIFY

"Feel like you have this opportunity, especially as a woman leader, to step into the leadership role and then treat yourself and your team with kindness."

—SARAH JONES SIMMER, COO, BUMBLE

"My first inclination is to give my opinion and squash everything. You can't do that as a leader. Let everybody put their opinions on the table. It's not about consensus; it's about getting the input and then making everybody feel like they've been heard, and not being the first to speak and squashing the discourse."

—MATT WOOL, PRESIDENT, ACCELERATION PARTNERS

"Hang on a little while. It's going to show up. You've just got to be patient. Keep putting yourself in the right position."

—RYAN MONTGOMERY, COO, CLICKFUNNELS

"Don't be a jackass. Leave your ego at the door. I've always been an athlete. I've always been a performing student. Early in my career I was like, 'We're number one. We're the best. That's all that matters. I'm the best.' What I realize now is that, even if my region is doing the greatest, a true leader is going up and talking to his colleague that is not doing as well and making sure you're helping them by being humble, being vulnerable, and allowing yourself to continue to grow."

—GRIFF LONG, COO, ORANGE THEORY FITNESS

"It's okay to change course, and you can figure it out. There are many resources out in the world that help you to grow and develop the skills that you want and not feel locked into one path because it's the path that you started out on."

—ERIN NELSON, COO, KINDRED BRAVELY

"I would try to convince myself that the authentic version of me is the best available version. I should accept whatever comes from that with grace. I shouldn't try to be someone else."

—MATT MACINNIS, COO, RIPPLING

"I was that girl who didn't believe she was bringing enough to the table. I over-studied, over-compensated. Some of that is what society and life feed you, particularly when you're a black woman in tech. I wish that I had bet on myself sooner."

—JANEEN UZZELL, COO, WIKIMEDIA

"Get out on the road. Try things. Be riskier."

—RICHARD URUCHURTU, VICE PRESIDENT
OF OPERATIONS, KLIENTBOOST

"You're a great problem solver. You're there to solve problems. Don't get upset about problems. That's what you do."

—THEO GOLDIN, COO, HINT WATER

"Don't worry about what choices you make. Don't be so focused on making good decisions about your career, but rather make the decisions based on your effort, your application of your disciplines and your excellence, and just make it happen."

—ANDY HALLIDAY, COO, LIFEAID

"Don't forget to have fun and be grateful."

—SUNIL RAJASEKAR, PRESIDENT AND CTO, MINDBODY

"Take more risks. Especially in the world of technology, there is such rapid change. Doing things that feel a little uncomfortable or a lot uncomfortable, that feel like, 'I have no idea how this is going to turn out,'—those have actually been some of the best experiences."

—ANNE RAIMONDI, COO, ASANA

ACKNOWLEDGEMENTS

- There are *so* many people who have made this book possible, and who have helped me build the COO Alliance and the *Second in Command* podcast. I'm going to try to thank you all. If I miss you, your name will appear in the first edits I do.
- To my amazing team at the COO Alliance: Meredith Kuba, my EA for almost seven years—*thank you* for packing my parachute. I can't imagine building this without you. To an amazing Jason Torres who runs all our tech and handles the entire podcast—I'm proud of you and the work you do every day. Jesse Brannon, we're just getting started together, but you're with me forever. Dustin Lockman, you're really making your mark here; thank you. Mandi Relyea-Voss and Emrys DeSousa, thanks for all things social media. And Boris Tsibelman, Matt Astifan, Matt Hunt, and all those on your teams, and the team at Hawke Media: thanks for helping me grow, and for working with me when I freak out with stress.
- To my more than 220 *Second in Command* podcast guests:

you've been like a real- world MBA. I've learned from all of you. I'm not going to list all of you. But I love the ones who share their episodes with their email lists and on social media just a little bit more than the others. ;)

- This book would not be as insightful and/or as effective at getting people to tell others to read it without these amazing humans who proofread the manuscript for suggestions, gaps, etc.: Lesley Steele, Lindsay Smith, Jeremy Knauff, Joe Polish, Parchelle Tashi, John Dalton, Hunter McMahon, Brian Beers, John Bowen, Chris Prenovost, Michael Erath, Craig Miller, Dominique Farnan, David Brickley, Billy Gene. And thanks also to the countless dozens of others who gave me title and cover suggestions.

- And my ongoing thanks to Jennifer Hudye, my partner on all things Vivid Vision® who is helping to ensure thousands of companies worldwide are using Vivid Visions instead of useless vision statements. She and her team at Conscious Copy helped me polish my Vivid Vision for the COO Alliance that you're reading in this book.

- And finally, a huge thank you to the team at Scribe for making this book a reality. It's no wonder it's now the fourth book I've done with you. And to the amazing Tim Cooke, who worked with me under crazy deadlines and timelines to help me pull all my ideas and content into such a powerful book: I loved working with you on this.

ABOUT THE AUTHOR

CAMERON HEROLD is "the COO Whisperer." He is founder of the COO Alliance and the Second in Command podcast. By age thirty-five, Cameron had helped build his first two $100 million companies. By forty-two, he had engineered 1-800-GOT-JUNK?'s spectacular growth from $2 million to $106 million in revenue in just six years.

An in-demand speaker, best-selling author, mentor, and coach, he has shown hundreds of clients globally how to double both their revenue and profit in three years or less. He is the top-rated lecturer at EO/MIT's Entrepreneurial Masters Program and a powerful speaker at entrepreneur and leadership events online and in-person globally.